Irresistible Businesses: Dazzling and Delighting Customers for Life!

Irresistible Businesses: Dazzling and Delighting Customers for Life!

Lynn M. Thomas

iUniverse, Inc.
New York Lincoln Shanghai

Irresistible Businesses:
Dazzling and Delighting Customers for Life!

iUniverse, Inc.

For information address:
iUniverse, Inc.
2021 Pine Lake Road, Suite 100
Lincoln, NE 68512
www.iuniverse.com

ISBN: 0-595-29719-6

Printed in the United States of America

To my beloved sister Kimmy, for her unswerving love, total acceptance and unstoppable belief in me. Even though you have died, the memory of our powerful, pure, and loving connection still gives me untold amounts of courage, perseverance and determination in the darkest of times. Thanks for the joy, fun, laughs and the rich, pure and beautiful memories that nurture my heart and soul.

ACKNOWLEDGEMENTS

Carolyn, for bringing abundant amounts of joy, silliness, laughter and love into my life.

Tracy, for being the "bestest" friend anyone could ever have. You are vitally important to me. Thanks for your glorious friendship, constant love and joyous belief in me!

Mom, for your unswerving devotion, unconditional love, fervent loyalty, and kind sweetness, as well as for always being there for me. Also, for your wonderful humor and for being a "Master Mom" from whom I learn a lot!

Dad, for your unquenchable zest and joy for life, passionate love of work, determined perseverance and buoyant resiliency despite life's circumstances. Thanks for being there for me and giving me your best!

Peter Rengel, for your boundless love, deep caring, and sweet and gentle guidance through many challenging times. I know I have never lost your love and that is really important to me. Additionally, for your rare and refreshing ability to rejoice with what is now, and for your overflowing love for your son and the way you model how to be a great parent!

Debbie, for the incredible depth of loving and caring you have shown for me and for my business, and for the selfless hours you generously offered to keep everything flowing so smoothly.

Jeff, my bro, for your selfless and dedicated work to help me with a major project, as well as your unending love and caring for me.

Philip, for being Kimmy's best friend and still loving her now, and for your trust in and caring for me. I love the gift of our friendship, the Kimmy stories we have shared, and the laughter, joy and fun.

Elliot, for deeply touching me with your pure love, gentle sweetness, complete innocence, kind honesty, abundant and joyful welcomes, and silly fun.

Joyce, for reaching out and caring about me, and for your willingness to keep our bond vibrant and alive.

Shelley, for being a witty, smart and sensitive sister-in-law.

Alex, for your wonderful blend of intelligence, kindness, inquisitiveness and caring.

Stan Dale, for creating HAI and for your passionate and timeless love!!!

Lisa Wright, for your undying friendship and for the many gifts of love you have given me along the way.

Lisa Wolf, for your "Exquisite Editing" of this book and for your love and caring friendship.

Chris McVicker, for being an early and raving fan of me and my work. Many, many thanks!

Roger Sitkins, for your generous honesty, caring and kind guidance in my work, and for caring about me and the rest of my life.

The Village, for your unbelievably generous caring, love and support, and your visits to help me raise Carolyn.

Steve Honyotski, for being with me when I got "the telephone call," and for your support afterwards; for your belief in me, my business, and my ideas; and for your continued support.

Wendy, for your assistance and gentleness in helping me complete this book.

CONTENTS

Part I

Irresistible Businesses: Dazzling and Delighting Customers for Life!

Introduction

Over the fourteen-plus years I have worked in the customer and employee loyalty and retention industry, I have been puzzled by one common management practice. Why don't more companies understand the fact that retention efforts generate higher profits than the common practice of repeatedly seeking new business? The latter usually takes years to produce a profit. Yes, every company needs new business, but when viewed from a profitability perspective, the excessive value placed on generating new business is financially unsound. The average company loses 20% of its customers every year. So to maintain the same profitability level, the company needs to generate 20% more new customers per year, while to grow, it must generate even more than that. That strains any business' resources—people, systems, goodwill and money. Yet year after year, one company after another continues to do the same things while expecting better results, but producing more-or-less the same results. People in these companies feel that they are doing their best, achieving the best they can. How frustrating! In this country, we lose 180 million customers a year!

Additionally, it costs most companies, on average, six to eight times more to obtain a new customer than to retain an existing customer. So, let's do some simple calculations. If an average customer generates $1,000 of profit each year, and will stay with a company for an average of ten years, then that customer would create $10, 000 of profit for the business. If the average company pays $4,000 in acquisition costs to attract a new customer, but $500 to retain an existing one, where should the company focus most of its resources? Yes, on retaining existing customers, because doing so will have a multiplying effect on profits: it will reduce operating costs and increase profits, as well as increasing the company's sales hit ratios.

In two to three years, a 5% increase in a company's retention rate will generate a 15% to 85% increase in profits. Tell me about another marketing or financial strategy that will generate this level of profitability. It is the most powerful leveraged opportunity in your company today. No doubts. No questions. No second thoughts. It is the winner, hands down.

This is the only book on the market that offers you the unique opportunity to take advantage of these powerful dynamics to improve your company's effectiveness and profitability. After completing the exercises in the Appendices, you will have a much better idea of the strengths and weaknesses of your firm, and you will be able to identify specific ways to improve on its strengths and minimize its weaknesses. Improving your understanding of the whys and hows of customer retention will allow your company to soar!

What is the Wow! Level?

BOTTOM LINE DEFINITION OF
"CUSTOMER RETENTION"

100%
PASSIONATE
commitment to
keep your
customers for
life.

In essence people buy only two things: a positive experience or the expectation of a positive experience. What does your business sell? What are your customers buying? All companies need to create a compelling buying experience that incorporates the elements of surprise and delight. Most companies do not develop products or services with this compelling buying experience as the ultimate goal. Thus, most companies' products and services are about average, producing average profits and average results. Being anything but the best does not work for me or for my clients. Second best is NOT an option.

Many people know that I am a bottom-line type of person, and when I start reading a book I do not want to have to wait until the middle or the end to understand the essence or core message of the book. So I will tell you my core message now and I will tell you up front. Customer retention is a choice. And it is only one of many choices you could make. Only you can make this choice for yourself. It is a 100% passionate commitment to keep your top customers for life! Period. End of story. There is no longer any gray area; there is no longer an option to do it 99% of the time. This must be done each and every day. To have a "Reality Check" on how customer-and employee-focused your company is, see Appendix 1.

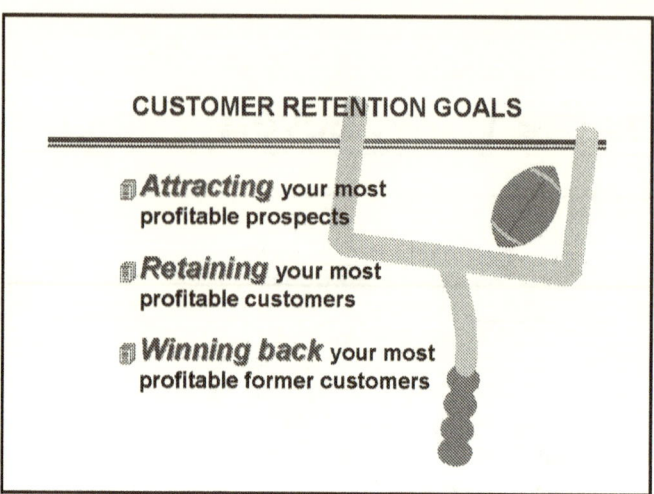

Customer retention is not well understood. Most people think it applies only to retaining a company's existing customers. The best approach to customer retention has three components. Number one, attract your most profitable prospects in a way that Wows! and delights them. Number two, work with your current, most profitable customers in a way that Wows! and delights them. Number three—the one most companies do not even see as a source of profitable new business—work with your most profitable former customers in a way that Wows! and delights them so they decide to come back and do business with your company again.

The purpose of marketing and sales must be to create a customer for life. Sales has two parts. The first is making the sale. The second (and often neglected) part is keeping the customer for life. Customer retention is about creating a customer for life, not just making a sale. It is about thinking of customers as ongoing, permanent clients, not just one-time purchasers of a product or service. There is an enormous difference between the two. Each of customer retention's three components needs to be carefully thought through, to ensure that a company has a strategy to maximize the opportunity to retain and replicate its most profitable customers at every juncture. Thus, to retain your "A" customers, you must know what "A" prospects need to become customers, what "A" customer need to become customers for life and what "A" former customers need to return and stay for life. What do "A" customers value most about doing business with you?

Each of the components of your customer retention goals is interconnected and synergistic. What information can each of these components provide that can make your company more effective in the other areas?

1. Knowing which of your existing customers become loyal can help you sharpen your prospecting by spending more time with those that will become more loyal, thereby attracting similar high-potential customers.
2. Knowing which customers have defected and why can help you sharpen your prospect targeting to avoid attracting prospects that are prone to defection.
3. Understanding new customers' needs enables you to better customize products and services to provide ever-increasing value to your customers.
4. Knowing which customers have defected and why can help with early detection of current customers who are at risk and allow you to intervene to prevent their defection.
5. Comparing the profiles of high-value prospects against lost customers can be helpful for identifying those lost customers worthy of winback efforts.

In order to achieve a 93% to 95% retention rate, each of these components needs to be analyzed.

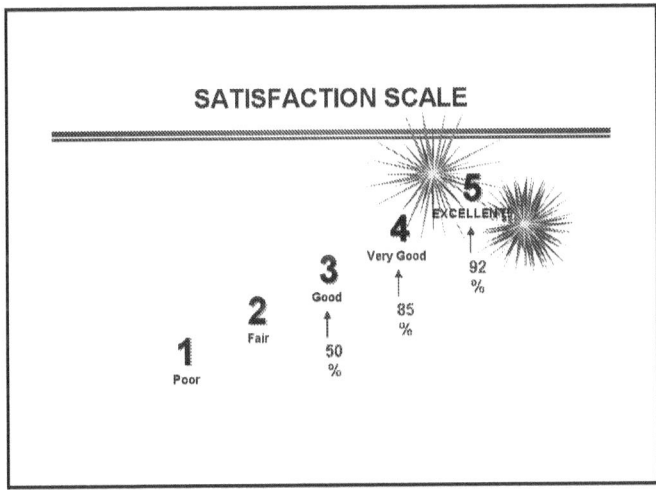

Some people have asked me why is it so important to Wow! customers. Why can we not just satisfy them? AT&T was doing some customer satisfaction research and keeping track of customer satisfaction levels when it was breaking up into the Baby Bells. It had a five-point satisfaction scale and it identified the people who said their level of satisfaction was "3" ("Good"), "4" ("Very Good"), or "5" ("Excellent"). Management lumped these customers together and called them satisfied. What puzzled senior management was that over 94% of its customers fell into those three categories, and the company was still losing market share. If customers are satisfied, why are they leaving?

The company tracked these customers for the next two to three years, and what management noticed astonished them. Of the customers that rated their satisfaction as "5," 92% were still with AT&T. Of those with a level of "4," only 85% still remained. Of those that rated their satisfaction as a "3," only 50% were still with the company.

This is the most powerful point. Satisfaction is an antiquated and ineffective way to predict current or future retention rates and profitability. In fact, mere satisfaction (a "3") has a ZERO correlation with retention. One-half of the customers calling themselves satisfied are as likely to leave as they are to stay.

Why Satisfaction Does Not Keep Customers

When I hear a company is striving to satisfy its customers, I cringe. Satisfaction does not retain customers in today's marketplace. It is true, satisfaction used to be enough. However, nowadays customers have become more sophisticated and have had many positive experiences with other companies. They are more demanding. The level of satisfaction that is necessary to "Wow!" and delight customers is "4.7" to "5" on a five-point scale. At these levels, these highly satisfied customers are **six times** more likely to repurchase, cross-buy and refer. That makes your job much easier and reduces your customer acquisition costs. Spending resources to achieve a satisfaction level less than "4.7" is not a financially wise investment. The Wow! level is what will make a difference. See the Appendices 2, 3, 4 and 5 for some examples of specific ways for your company to start to Wow! its top customers.

Raving fans will rate their satisfaction 4.7 to 5.0. Loyal customers are found at 4.4; indifferent customers hover around 4.2, and customers who are about to defect rally around 3.7. These figures shock most people. Most people think that being rated a "4" on a five-point scale is quite an accomplishment. On the surface, it does appear to be an accurate perception. But once you probe further into the numbers and look at retention, it becomes blatantly obvious that this level does not retain customers. What level of satisfaction characterizes your top customers?

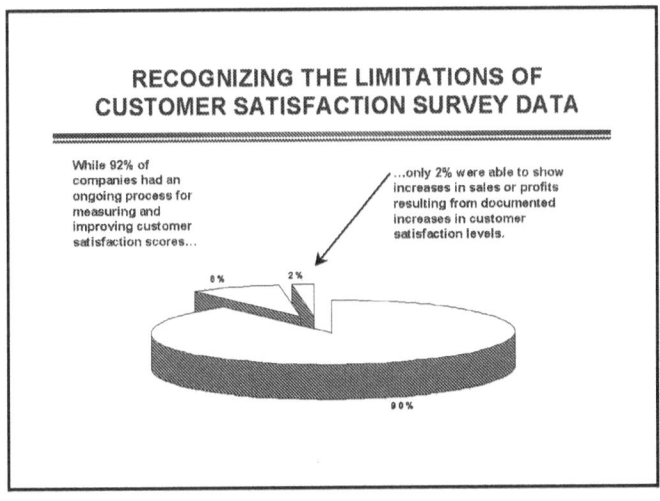

RECOGNIZING THE LIMITATIONS OF CUSTOMER SATISFACTION SURVEY DATA

While 92% of companies had an ongoing process for measuring and improving customer satisfaction scores...

...only 2% were able to show increases in sales or profits resulting from documented increases in customer satisfaction levels.

That may be why the Corporate Executive Bureau in Washington, D.C., which works with the Fortune 1000 companies, found that while 92% of those companies had an ongoing process for measuring and improving customer satisfaction scores, only 2%—that is right, only 2%—could document any increase in sales or profits as a result of this process. Now, these are some of the best-run companies in the country. They have resources to hire the brightest and the best to conduct and analyze market research and they hire the best consultants to analyze the results. What is not working?

One of the answers is that satisfaction is an outdated and ineffective method of generating increases in sales, profits or retention. It used to work. In the 1970s and 1980s, satisfaction was adequate to keep customers with companies. Then we started to hear about product quality, then customer service, and then customer loyalty. Eventually, I predict, companies will be measuring customer retention because it is the proven driver of long-term profitability. If a company were keeping 93% to 95% of its most profitable customers, much would have to go wrong for the company to fail to generate a healthy profit every year.

Thus, these companies got poor results for their investment, because they created customer surveys that asked questions that are indicators of satisfaction, not retention. What is the difference? Retention is behaviorally driven, whereas satisfaction is attitudinally driven.

Why didn't measuring satisfaction work as a tool to predict retention rates? One expert gives his version of what is occurring in companies that measure satisfaction. "Most organizations have some form of customer satisfaction measurement, and in most cases it is close to useless. It is not timely, does not link back to practical results and to the people who have to take action to achieve those results, and does not link to the financial bottom line. You have to have a loop."

Another reason measuring satisfaction did not work was that **none** of these companies identified what was most important to their customers. They did what most companies do, and generated the contents of their survey or questionnaire **internally**, thus excluding the customers' input. This is a crucial error, which will keep a company blinded to about 40% of the reasons customers come to, stay with or leave an organization. See Appendices 6 and 7 for examples of how customer loyalty builds profits, and a superb analysis of the limitations of satisfaction survey data.

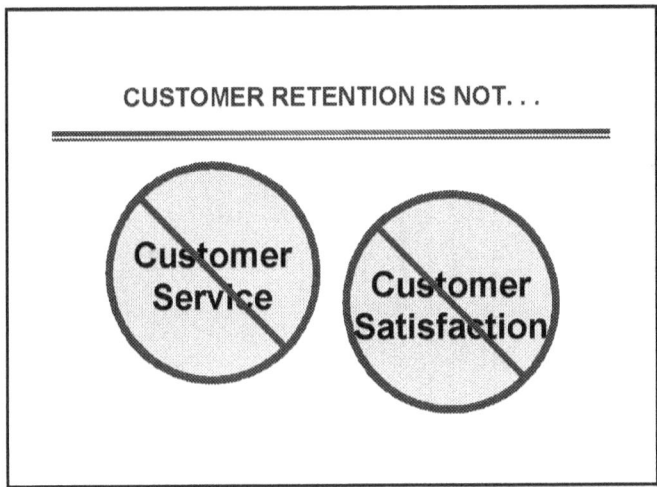

Satisfaction measures the frequency rather than the severity of a complaint. In other words, satisfaction surveys do not determine how likely a customer is to leave because of a complaint. Thus, for example, if 20% of a company's customers complained about the long telephone wait time, and this was the factor with the highest percentage of customer complaints, it would seem logical that the company needs to reduce its wait time. However, the survey has failed to ask the key question, "What level of severity did the customer assign to the long wait time?" In essence, how important is it to the customer's decision-making process that the wait time be reduced? I have yet to find a company that asks the customers about both the quality of their experience and its importance, in order to capture the information needed to develop the best initiatives for generating the highest retention rates possible.

Most companies lump all their customers into one customer pool for customer surveys. However, it is vitally important for companies to segment their customers into at least three tiers, "A," "B" and "C." In this book, you will learn the vital importance of segmentation to a successful retention effort. Since the "A"s represent 20% of the customers that generate 80% of the revenue, in customer satisfaction surveys where the "A," "B" and "C" customers are not differentiated, the "A"s are far outnumbered by the "B"s and "C"s. This leads to customer satisfaction survey results that are not adequately specific to "Wow!" the customers that every company should be most interested in Wow!ing. In such surveys, the two least profitable customer segments' needs dominate the data, and that prevents companies from learning what they most need to know: what their most profitable customers want, and how to deliver it to them superbly each and every time to create a compelling buying experience.

Many people have asked me about the relationships among satisfaction, loyalty and retention. High levels of satisfaction are generated when a customer has positive experiences with a company. Then, as a satisfied customer, this person has additional positive experiences, which can create a loyal customer. Finally, when a loyal customer has had numerous positive experiences, that customer becomes a customer for life.

The difference between loyalty and retention is that the latter usually involves an emotional bond or an emotional dimension to the relationship. Most companies do not realize that emotions underlie people's decisions to buy initially, as well as their likelihood of developing loyalty.

The High Cost of a Revolving Door

STOP THE REVOLVING DOOR

Every month as customers and employees leave, 2.6% of your gross revenue walks out the door!

Every month, the average company sees 2.6% of its gross revenue walk out its door: 1.6% goes with customers and 1% goes with employees. This revolving door must be stopped!

Frederick Reichheld gives a great summary of the situation and its impact on our lives: "There is a retention crisis—and it is getting worse. The resulting churn is wreaking havoc on our lives, our businesses, and our economy. Like it or not, the average company loses half its customers every five years, half its employees every four years and half its investors every year. This churn has to stop!" Just think of the pressure this constant loss places on a company's people, resources, and systems. It is an enormous drain. It astonishes me that management is not jumping up and down and saying, "Wait a minute! We need to stop doing what we are doing that creates this mass exodus year after year."

In fact, 180 million customer-business affiliations are lost each year. That is a costly loss. The most common reason customers leave is the feeling of neglect or lack of appreciation from their current company. Is your company customer-focused? If not, what are most important steps to becoming customer-focused? See Appendices 8, 9, 10 and 11 for the "Ten Commandments of Being Customer-Focused;" also included are examples of the cost of poor service.

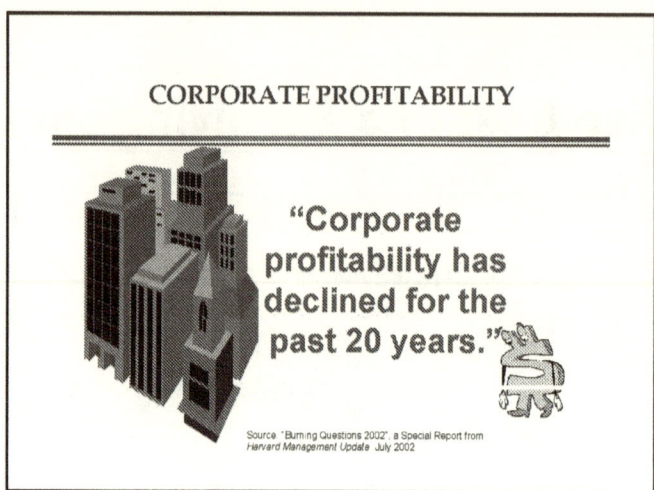

Because of all this, one can understand at least one of the reasons that corporate profitability has been declining for the past twenty years. Amazing as it may seem, a key underlying reason is that companies are not measuring the correct financial and marketing variables—they are more focused on satisfaction than retention, and thus are missing the critical link between retention, sales and profits.

The reality is that there is only one boss—the customer! When the customer leaves, s/he in essence is firing the company. How many customers fired your company last year? How much revenue did they take with them? Most people do not know these answers off the top of their heads, yet if I were to ask them their sales last year, more would know that number. What I propose is that your attention and resources be focused primary on retention, because it will more quickly and predictably increase your company's profitability than will any other activity your company can undertake.

The Powerful Upside Potential of Customer Retention

For every ___% increase in a business' Customer Retention Rate, its profits will increase ___%.

The power behind customer retention is understood by only a few. It is an outside-of-the-box strategy for long-term profitability. If the average company improves its retention rate by 5%, its profits will increase by 15% to 85%. I call this the Big Bang of retention. If you increase your sales by 5%, your bottom line will only increase by about 5%. If you decrease costs by 5%, your bottom line will only increase by about 5%.

What is it about customer retention that it produces this multiplying effect? What happens when a customer is retained? First, you do not have to pay the high acquisition costs of replacing the customer. Second, the customer will most likely purchase additional services and products. Third, the customer may send referrals. Fourth, the company's operating costs for the customer decrease since the customer is more familiar with how the company works.

The degree of the impact that retention will have on the bottom line depends on two factors: the costs of acquiring new customers and the frequency of the sales churn.

The industries with the four highest acquisition costs, in order, are the insurance industry, banking, automobile sales, and travel and lodging. See

Appendix 12 for some of the obvious—and less obvious—costs of customer acquisition.

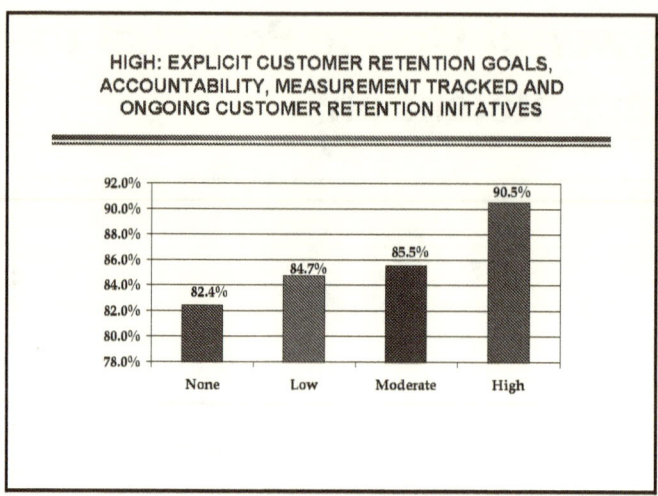

Companies that have the following four items in place achieve higher retention rates:

1.   Explicit retention goals
2.   Accountability
3.   Tracking and measuring of customer retention
4.   Ongoing customer retention initiatives

If none of these is in place, the retention rate will be 82.4%. With a low level of emphasis on customer retention, the retention rate increases to 84.7%. With a moderate level of emphasis, the rate rises to 85.5%, while with a high level of emphasis it jumps to 90.5%. Retention efforts pay off handsomely with a typical ROI of fifteen to one over four to five years.

MOMENT OF TRUTH (MOT)

A *specific* incident a
customer uses to form a
general perception of the
quality and services of your
entire business.

"Moments of Truth" are very powerful contacts with a company that result in a customer deciding to come, stay with or leave that company. The term "Moments of Truth" comes from the book of the same name by Jan Carlzon. He purchased SAS airlines in 1979, an airline which had lost $30 million in the previous two years. In one year, he turned it around to make a profit of one million dollars. That is like turning the Titanic on a dime. What he discovered is that many customers would fly with them once, but not return again. Customers gave the usual reasons to the usual surveys. During a customer defection analysis that asked questions that probed deeply underneath their first or second responses, the company learned that customers did not feel the airplanes were safe. This puzzled the company, since it had not had any incidents of mechanical problems or anything else to indicate that the airplanes were not well maintained. When the interviewer continued to ask questions to four or five deeper levels, he uncovered the reason: Coffee stains had not been wiped up from the trays on the airplanes. When the passengers saw the coffee stains, they experienced a gut-level fear, and thought, "I hope they maintain the engines better." Most concluded that the company probably did not, and thus they did not fly with SAS again.

Notice that it was coffee stains on the trays: a very specific piece of data. It was not that the bathrooms were messy or the flight attendants were rude or there were cookie crumbs on the tray, but coffee stains. Jan Carlzon then became passionate about uncovering all of SAS's coffee stains, which represented their customers' "Moments of Truth." He claims that by managing the coffee stains and not the people, he was able to turn the company around in one year.

Coffee stains are more powerful than first impressions. In 1979, a passenger would have had many contacts with employees of SAS: making a reservation, checking baggage, getting a boarding pass. Yet, even if all of these were positive contacts, they could not outweigh the impact of **one** negative Moment of Truth: a coffee stain on the tray.

So, I ask you, where are your company's coffee stains? They are usually in places that we would not think of. You see, it is not what you know that is hurting your company's profits, but what you do not know. In a way, we are hunting to find the key coffee stains that are opening the exit doors for customers to easily leave your company. By nature, we human beings are loyal. I know you are not thinking, "I hope my doctor, dentist or car dealer really messes up so I can use the precious little time I have to find a replacement." Believe me, your customers do not want to leave your company. Yet the way your company interacts with them literally chases them out the open exit doors.

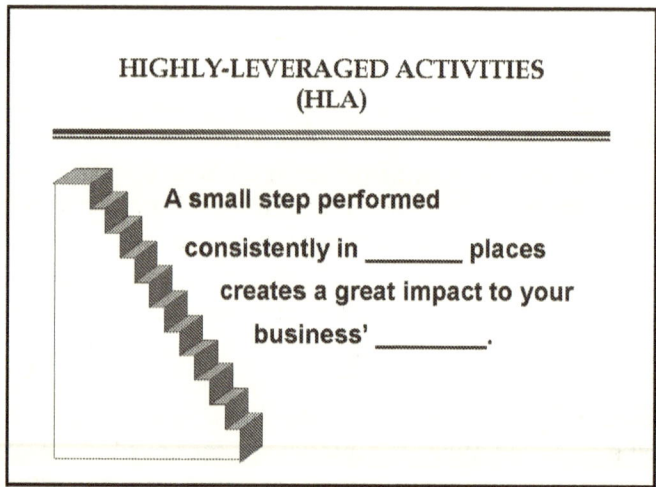

I have been privileged to work for a large and well-known hotel chain. The first hotel I worked with was located in Cambridge, Massachusetts. The hotel manager wanted to understand why the hotel's best customers, who were business travelers, did not return at a higher rate. As I do with all of my market research programs, in this study, I wanted to gather as many perspectives as possible in the qualitative stage so I could develop a powerful quantitative survey that would produce a high response rate, and specific and implementable results.

I started by interviewing the employees to uncover why they thought some customers did return. There were three common reasons: the hotel had a magnificent, newly-renovated lobby; it was the only hotel in the Boston area with an Olympic-sized swimming pool; and the hotel is located in Cambridge and not Boston, and some people prefer to not stay in the city. These all seemed plausible to me.

However, when I interviewed some of the hotel's best customers, I kept hearing stories about C.J. and Andrew. Who do you think they were? They were not the bellhops or the front desk staff. They were the doormen. However, these two men were no ordinary doormen. They had a phenomenal memory for names and faces. Thus, if anyone stayed at the hotel and returned within four to five years, C.J. and Andrew would greet them by name. But the most highly leveraged activity that they consistently did was to ask questions in order to customize the hotel's services to meet each customer's needs as best as they could.

The stories I heard were truly acts of customer love. Each morning, these two men would arrive 90 minutes early and scrub the circular driveway of the hotel. When I asked why, they responded, "Why not? We want everything to be perfect for our guests."

Every morning they would ask a new guest, "How did you sleep?" Let's say a guest responded, "Well, to tell you the truth, my neck is sore because the pillow was too hard, and the steak at your restaurant had too much gristle." They would profusely apologize to the disappointed guest. But they would go much further than that! What would they do with this information? They would keep note cards to record customer's preferences. That evening when the disappointed guest returned, he would find a softer pillow on his bed and a note saying, "Courtesy of C.J. and Andrew. We hope you have a better night's sleep." Further, C.J. and Andrew would call the restaurant and let the manager know that if this guest were to order steak, the steak must not have any gristle. When the guest checked out, he would be given credit for the steak, and if he had complained a lot, he would get credit for the entire meal. Pretty amazing!

One woman said that every time she opened the ironing board she would run her stockings. So when she checked in to her room, the ironing board would already be open. Another woman had come to town for her daughter's wedding. It had begun to rain about fifteen minutes before she arrived at the hotel. She was disappointed that her car would have some raindrop marks on it. During the night, C.J. and Andrew arranged to have her car washed and cleaned. It delighted this woman to no end!

Do you think the Four Seasons or the Ritz Carlton could win these guests? No way! They are very loyal, and are raving fans of the hotel.

There are seven specific activities that are known to produce great results when done consistently. Most companies do not do these activities frequently enough. The seven highly leveraged activities are:

- Planning
- Goal setting
- Training
- Market research and development
- Organizing
- Streamlining communication
- Giving and receiving feedback

The nature of these activities is that they provide a company and its managers with direction and focus. The clearer the direction and the stronger the focus, the more successful the company will become. When you are engaging in these activities, the results will consistently be greater than if you were engaging in other activities. Following the 20/80 rule, you should spend 80% of your time in these highly leveraged activities.

There are only three things any company needs to do to be highly profitable. Know who are your best customers, focus on retaining them and be willing to break out of your mindset. As human beings, we find the latter very difficult to do. Tom Peters said that it is much easier to destroy a company than to change it. Why is that? A company's success has been built on certain beliefs or perceptions, and the company's leaders are very emotionally invested in maintaining the status quo. Certain perceptions or beliefs are accepted as true, and people do not even question them. In fact, the longer a person has been in an industry or with a company, the less likely it is that the person will be the source of new ideas or approaches. The odds are that he or she will be the last to change! See Appendices 13 and 14 for tips for high customer retention rates, and how to pinpoint your company's "Moments of Truth."

So when you are looking at your company, take a broad view and be a detective looking for your coffee stains. They could be in the company's products and services, its distribution channel, the employee benefits and compensation, or customer service. Do your best to be objective about where the coffee stains are.

Most companies that I have worked with lack a clear and sharply defined mission or purpose that they are willing to stay committed to for a few years to reap the results. Without knowing where you want to go, you will probably end up in unfamiliar territory. You are like a sailboat without a rudder.

So, you need to know precisely who are your best customers, what they want from you, and a how to superbly deliver it to them each and every time. Period. Every successful company starts with this knowledge. Then, over time, companies will broaden their products and services, and lose the focus that made them successful early on. If you lack this focus, you will have products and services that are not highly valued by your customers, you will have frustrated employees since they will not be seeing the results of their efforts, and you will have valued customers leaving. The churn is already starting and will continue to drain your profits until focus and resources are utilized to slow it down.

Getting Down to Reality—the Implementation Steps

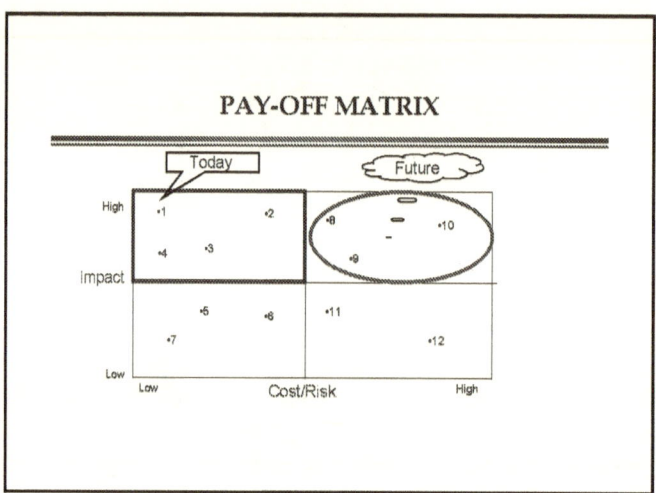

This payoff matrix illustrates the possible results of a market research project. There are some initiatives that will have a high impact and have a low risk and a low cost. These are the ones to implement today. The ones with a high impact but high risk and/or high costs need to be analyzed further. Those with a low impact and high costs are not currently options. Those with a low impact and low costs need to be further examined for possible implementation.

This matrix is very helpful for my clients in selecting the initiatives that will produce the highest ROI.

The New Business Realities Which Drive the Market

Some important new business realities are driving the pressing need for companies to be constantly flexible in order to change and to meet the market's demands. The first is that technology is driving the changes in the market. When it now costs $1/20^{th}$ of what it cost last year to capture a piece of data, technology becomes more available to all companies and all people.

Second, there is a limited supply of "A" customers. These are the 20% of your customer base which produce 80% of your revenue. In the 1980s and halfway through the 1990s, when a customer would leave, I would hear people say, "There are a lot more customers out there like that one." It may have been true in those days, although I doubted it then. We all know for sure that in this decade, each "A" customer is worth his/her weight in gold. They are very difficult and expensive to replace. One of my clients says, "It is not an option for an "A" client to leave this firm." You competition covets your "A" customers; invest in them to retain them, since you have already invested a significant amount of time and money to attract them. Be willing to do what it takes to keep them for life.

The third new business reality is that time is becoming a more precious commodity. For some people, more time-off is as valuable as a raise. When I am speaking to a corporate audience, I will ask, "How many people have more free time today than they did five years ago?" I rarely get a hand raised, and when I do, it is usually someone who is retiring. This is good news for you in your quest to retain your customers. Why? Because your customers do not have any more free time than you do—they have virtually none. Thus, they do not have the time to recreate the relationship they have with you. The better you know your customers' needs and preferences, the more they rely on you, and the harder it is for them to replace you. Since by nature we are loyal and by nature we do not like change, this lack of free time works in your favor. So the next time a customer says, "I am so busy," see this as the opportunity it is. S/he does not have time to replace you. This is good news! For customers to leave, companies really need to chase them out their open doors.

Other the other hand, how many people have stood in front of a microwave oven and felt impatient? Almost everyone has had this experience. Customers want speed, and you can never be fast enough. Soon, irrationally, we will want our vendors to anticipate what we want before we even know.

There are three currencies: speed, accuracy and expertise. In all industries, people are willing to pay extra for these. In the final analysis, all of these come down to time. If you are accurate, I do not have to spend my time calling you to correct a mistake. If you are an expert in my business, I do not have to take the time to explain my business to you.

Fourth, the buying cycle has become perpetual. In the past in some industries, competitors would only approach your customers at certain time, e.g. renewal period. Today, your competitors are in constant contact with your "A" and "B" customers. Thus, you need to build closer relationships with these customers.

Fifth, mass customization is replacing mass production. Five years ago, Seiko made 25 watchbands. Today they make 3,000. They have identified that they have 3,000 different types of customers, and they are making a watchband for each customer. That is one-to-one marketing: one watch for each type of customer.

Mass customization is all around us. Take M&M's. When I was a child, there was one brown package for M&M's. Today there are dozens of different packages. When I was a child, one pair of sneakers was all I needed. Today, if anyone thinks s/he can walk and run in the same pair of sneakers, s/he is out-of-date. The footwear companies have sneakerized us. Levis pants have never really fit women well. Only 28% of women could buy Levis off the rack and have them fit well. Now you can go into a genuine Levis store and get your measurements taken, and a few days later, for $20 more, you can receive custom-made Levis. One-to-one marketing is here to stay!

Sixth, customer relationships are the new, and only lasting, competitive advantage. Most companies' products and services are commodities, so the depth and breath of the relationships that the company has with its customers is the glue that will keep that customer with the company for life. To the best of your ability, each of you must become a C.J. or an Andrew. Know your "A" customers' preferences. Record them. Act on them. Understand your "A" customers wants better than anyone else does. Cater to them and they will stay with you. Since no one else knows their needs and preferences as well as you, no one can be as terrific at delivering the experience they want each time. For some outstanding questions to ask customers in order to customize your service to Wow! them, see Appendices 15 and 16.

Learning to do things differently is not easy. It takes persistence, and persistence is a priceless commodity in today's business world. When children are attempting to walk, what happens when they fall down? They get back up again, and again, and again, and again, until they learn to walk. They are willing to fall on their diaper many times before they walk. Now take a look at us adults. We try something new once, or maybe, if we are big risk takers, twice, and if we are not good at it, we say "Forget it." Where did we get the idea that the first or second time we attempt to do something new, we should be good at it? If that had been true of us in our infancy, many of us would still be crawlers, speaking baby talk!

It can sometimes be inspiring to look at some of the world's greatest leaders or inventors, the obstacles they had to overcome, and their raw high level of pure persistence. Take Thomas Edison. After he had made 5,000 attempts to invent the electric light bulb, a young journalist interviewed him. He asked Mr. Edison, "Why do you persist in attempting to invent an electric light bulb when the great minds of today say it is impossible?" Mr. Edison replied, "Young man, you do not understand how the universe works. I have identified 5,000 ways that do not work. That puts me 5,000 ways closer to the one that will." It was on his 10,028th attempt that he succeeded. How many of us would even try one thousand times to create something? Very few.

Colonel Sanders personifies another great story about the relationship between persistence and success. When he retired and received his first Social Security check, he looked at the amount and said, "This is no way to live." He asked himself, "What do I do really well?" and responded, "I make great fried chicken." He decided he would go to a restaurant and would offer his recipe, stipulating that he would get half of the additional money that the restaurant made from using his fried chicken recipe. He went to the first restaurant, and spoke with the owner. After listening to Colonel Sanders, the owner dismissed him, saying, "I already have a fried chicken recipe." Colonel Sanders went to another restaurant and was turned down in a similar fashion. He went to the next one, and the next one. The 1,016[th] restaurant said OK, and that was the beginning of Kentucky Fried Chicken.

Babe Ruth held the record for many years of having hit the most home runs, but he also had had the most strikeouts. Abraham Lincoln's road to the White House was fraught with failures.

Walt Disney is also another great story. At age 40, he was broke and suffered a nervous breakdown. After he recovered, he started the company—the empire—that bears his name.

Most of us give up much too soon in attempting to learn or master something new. Bring forth that young part of you that could do anything, that is undaunted by setbacks, and watch what that attitude will do to your rate of success.

The New and Promising Relationship Paradigm

There is a new paradigm, which has emerged to dominate the marketplace. The old set of rules was you only needed to be responsive; now, customers want you to anticipate their needs. Oh, those demanding customers! We used to have the three-minute relationship. "Hi, how are you and your family?" Now, every interaction needs to be nurturing and a sales opportunity. You need to gather data to understand your customers' needs and preferences.

VALUE OF CUSTOMER RETENTION RELATIONSHIPS PARADIGM CHANGE

In a world that focuses on Customer Retention, a number of differences are apparent:

Instead of . . .	Customer Retention
Focusing on products...	Focuses on customers
Measuring and valuing transactions...	Measures and values relationships
Looking at a single financial year...	Looks at profits and value over several years
Basic services	Value-added services

Products and services used to attract and even retain customers. Now, the depth and the breath of your relationship with the customer is the only lasting competitive advantage. You each need to be a C.J. or an Andrew.

Satisfaction used to work. Now, clients want to be delighted and Wow!ed. Resolving each issue as it arose used to be adequate; now, customers seek employees who are knowledgeable, and that is what sustains the relationships. The focus used to be on service and mass production. Now, it is on keeping customers for a lifetime because of their lifetime value. No customer should need to give a company his/her preferences more than once. The information must be captured and kept in the customer's portfolio.

The customer has become more sophisticated and demanding, and over time, what is necessary to keep a customer has radically changed.

When companies decide to focus on customer retention, a number of variables in the relationship need to change. First, the focus has moved from products to customers. Companies will have fewer product managers and more customer managers. The goal is to obtain the greatest share of the customer's wallet. You have this very profitable customer—how can you meet his or her needs? What new products are necessary? What a contrast with the old perspective: "I have this new product; how many customers can I sell it to?"

Secondly, we used to measure and value transactions; now, we measure and value relationships.

Third, we used to look at the revenue a customer would generate for a single financial year; now, we want to know the lifetime value of the revenue.

Fourth, customers used to be satisfied with basic services; now, they want and expect to receive value-added services. In summary, the former ways of interacting with customers was to focus on the products and sell them in a transaction; customers' value was measured by the dollars they generated in a single financial year while the company provided basic services. Now the focus has shifted to creating customer relationships for a lifetime by adding value. This is a major difference that significantly impacts almost ever area of a company. How have you and your company changed to meet this new paradigm?

The Icarus Paradox is based on the mythological character of Icarus. Icarus' father gave him a set of wings, held together with wax, so he could fly. He also gave his son one warning, which was to not fly too close to the sun. In his exuberance, the son flew too close to the sun, his wings melted and he fell to the earth. His fatal flaw was trying to soar too far. So, you may be asking, why am I relating this story to you in a book about customer and employee retention? Well, there are many examples of cases when companies are flying high, and their success blinds them to the need to change. Thus, many companies' unique competitive advantages became their downfall, because the companies saw their competitive advantages as the one and only way to do the business. The stronger the company's competitive advantage and the longer the company has followed "the way" to do business, the more likely it is that this very success will lead to an equal or greater failure. The more successful a company has been, the more likely it is that the company is a candidate for an Icarus Paradox.

This phenomenon is best illustrated by looking at the first significant book written on quality in the business world, *In Search of Excellence* by Tom Peters and Robert Waterman, Jr. in 1982. It reported on 43 of the "best-run" companies in America. It is fascinating that within five years, only fourteen of those companies were still financially solvent. The reason, according to a *Business Week* study, was that they "failed to react and respond to change."

The bigger question is why. Why were they more likely than other companies to fail to react and respond to change? Because they had been heralded into the spotlight and been deemed to be the benchmark, "the way." Because of that, they did not perceive the need to change, but rested on their laurels, and the rest is history. As Tom Peters says, "It is easier to destroy a company than it is to change it."

So, some of you are with a company that has been very successful, maybe even one that represents "the way" your industry should do business. You are the most likely candidates for an Icarus Paradox, so be very vigilant to new developments. Read trade publications in other industries, as well as magazines about topics you know little about. This will keep you on the cutting edge. "When the pace of change inside an organization is slower than the pace of change outside an organization, the end is near." Make sure that your company is keeping up. If you do not take the time to understand the forces of change, your competitors will. You can count on it. There are only about 25 companies that have mastered staying profitable and being excellent at their business. It is a rarity. See Appendix 17 for a listing of some of the companies that are best at customer service.

The Power of Paradigms and Mastering Change with Grace

An organization must change—it simply must—if it is to prosper. Rather than banging your head against the wall of hard reality and bruising your spirit, invest your energy in making quick adjustments. Each day, every person needs to improve how s/he does his/her job in one small way. As I mentioned earlier, when the pace of change inside an organization is slower than the pace of change outside an organization, the end is near. Who is in charge of the pace of change inside an organization? You are. So it is your responsibility, to yourself and to your career, to make quick daily adjustments. After all, in this marketplace, you are in charge of your career. The days are gone when you could rely on management to manage your career. It is Your Name, Inc.

Change is constantly happening around us. Take the railroad industry. In 1920 it had two million workers; today, it has 231,000. In 1990, there were 109,000 carriage and harness markers, while today there are so few, they do not show up on the census. In 1910, there were over 11.5 million farm workers, while today we have 891,000. On the other hand, look at the number of jobs that have been created by inventions and changes as others have been destroyed by the same forces. Airline pilots and mechanics: in 1900 there were none, but today there are 232,000. Similarly with medical technicians: in 1910 the profession did not exist, while today there are 1.3 million. In 1900 there were no truck drivers, bus drivers, or taxi drivers, while today they number over 3.3 million. Thus, the cycle of destruction and creation of jobs and new industries through changes and inventions is not static, but dynamic, and it surely will remain so into the future.

Another way to look at the accelerated pace of change is to look at production speed. In 1990, it took six years for an automobile to go from concept to production. Today, it takes two years. Most of Hewlett-Packard's current revenues come from products that did not exist a year ago. Ninety percent of Miller Brewing Company's revenues come from beers that did not exist 24 months ago. Thus, even with industries that have been around for many decades, the pace of change has accelerated, demanding that everyone find better and faster ways to produce their services and products. It is natural for most people to resist change, but there are techniques to overcome most of the common pitfalls. See Appendices 18, 19 and 20 for some excellent material on people's resistance to change.

We all have blind spots in looking into the future and assessing what new products and services will be the most successful. This is part of being a human being. No one can see from all perspectives. We all have filters through which we see our world. We have lots of company! In 1927, Harry Warner of Warner Brothers said, "Who the hell wants to hear actors talk?" Why did he make that comment? Because silent movies were the rage, and there was minimal interest in the "talkies." In 1943, Thomas Watson, Chairman of IBM, said, "I think there is a world market for about five computers." He was off by many factors of ten!

For decades, it was a known medical fact that no human being could run a mile in less than four minutes. Roger Bannister, an English medical school student, did it in 1954, and within three years, ten people followed suit. I personally believed any of those ten people could have been Roger Bannister, but they were only able to do it after he did. Why? Because most of us live our lives in a narrow world of what we believe is possible, "The Possible World." The impossible, or what we think is impossible, does not even appear on our radar screen.

There is another whole universe of activities (our "Impossible World") that does not receive our attention or focus. Why should anyone spend time focusing on what everyone knows is impossible? There is a good reason: new ideas always start to emerge on the fringes. Just think about the mid-1990s. It was impossible to conceive that the Internet could become such an integral part of business, and almost nobody could imagine Palm Pilots, voice recognition software, or cellular telephones. We do not even strive to attain a goal that lies in that "Impossible World," since we believe we would fail. Then we are stunned when a new, "impossible" invention hits the marketplace.

Thus, most people live their lives in a comfortable box or "comfort zone." We drive to work the same way every day, eat with the same people, go to the same restaurants, shop at the same stores, spend our time with the same people, read the same magazines…and we wonder why we do not get new ideas. We just keep doing the same things over and over, thinking that feeling comfortable is a desirable situation. Actually, feeling uncomfortable is more desirable for those who value innovation. Choose it much more frequently, and many new and refreshing ideas will enter your mind.

Joel Barker, author of *Paradigms: The Business of Discovering the Future,* says that the most important question to ask—and to ask frequently—is, "What is impossible to do today, but if it were possible, would fundamentally change our business?" Ask this of your industry, your company, your department, yourself. This will take people to the edges of their "Impossible Worlds," and will reduce the odds that we will be blind-sided by the next unforeseen change. See Appendices 21 and 22 for some key observations about paradigms and the steps to uncovering your company's paradigms.

Read this sentence to yourself once. What does it say? Did you read it as "I love Paris in the springtime"? No, look at it again. It says, "I love Paris in the the springtime." Most of you missed the second "the." Why? How many "the"s have you seen in your lifetime? Thousands! So why did you miss this one? The fact is that our brains are designed to keep us **comfortable**, not to show us reality. Your brain started to read the sentence and jumped to the conclusion that it knew what the sentence said. Thus, you did not **really** read it.

Make the sound of the letter "F" out loud. Now read the following sentence silently to yourself and count the number of "F"s you see.

```
FINISHED FILES ARE
THE RESULT OF YEARS
OF SCIENTIFIC
RESEARCH OF A FEW
DEDICATED PEOPLE
```

How many "F"s did you see? Was it three, four, five, six, seven or eight? When I do this exercise with large groups, the majority of people see between four and six. There are actually seven "F"s in the sentence.

How many "F"s have you seen in your lifetime? You have probably seen millions.

```
FINISHED FILES ARE
THE RESULT OF YEARS
OF SCIENTIFIC
RESEARCH OF A FEW
DEDICATED PEOPLE
```

So why did you miss some here? Again, your brain filtered your perceptions, selecting the ones that sound like an "F." Most likely, you missed the ones that sound like a "V," i.e. the "F"s in "of." Again, remember that your brain wants to keep you comfortable: its goal is not to be accurate. We all have filters working all the time to screen out what might make us uncomfortable.

These simple illustrations show how it is possible for ten people to see a car accident occur and have ten different versions of what happened. No one is lying; each person saw it through his or her own individual filters, and thus each one has a different perspective.

There are new and better ways to do our work and live our lives, and we do not even see them, because we are as blinded to them as most of you were to the second "the" and all seven "F"s. We all live in our comfort zone or our "world of the possible." I strongly recommend doing one uncomfortable thing each day. Being uncomfortable pushes us to grow, as surprising as it may seem. Think again of babies learning to walk. They are not comfortable, but they persist, over and over again. They rarely cry when they fall. It is clear that they are driven to walk, and eventually they do. The more new and different experiences you have, the larger the tool box you will have to address new challenges in your work and life.

Mix things up in life and have fun! Go to a new restaurant, meet new people, do a new activity or sport, read a magazine that you know nothing about, be curious about life, in contrast to the attitude many of us have: "I have learned what I need to know and that is the end of my learning." As I observe people, I notice most do not smile, look happy, or even look alive as they walk around in life; they look rather blank. The infusion of new experiences will revitalize a person and engage more of a person's brain than s/he is used to, and then, watch out, World!

Henry Ford said it best: "If you think you can, or you think you can't, you are probably right." What I have noticed is that when I believe I can do something and have the confidence in myself, more likely than not I can achieve it. When I lack confidence, I rarely achieve my goal. I encourage you to eliminate the following words from your vocabulary, since they will limit the goals you can achieve. All these words are limiting and will keep you and your ides within your possible world.

- Impossible
- I'll try
- If only
- Ought
- Difficult
- I hope
- But
- Should
- I can't
- I have to
- However
- Doubt
- Hard
- I wish
- Wrong
- Fear

For example, have you ever noticed that the people who say they will **try** to make it to a party, never get there? In the immortal words of *Star Wars'* wise master Yoda, "There is no **try**; there is only **do** or **not do**!" Use words to empower your thoughts and actions!

Are you aware that you have voices inside your head? I am not talking about mental illness. Some of us have voices and some have committees, depending on how we were raised. Usually these internal voices are not very encouraging; they can be quite judgmental, and even downright cruel. In general, we are quite hard on ourselves. If any one of us were to treat a friend the way we treat ourselves, we would probably not have a single friend. We are critical, and will dwell for hours or days on a small mistake, while missing or dismissing all the positive activities we did in the meantime. Most people have a distorted, negative image of themselves. I implore you to quiet these voices. Thank them for sharing, then fill yourself with positive talk and surround yourself with positive people. One's attitude strongly correlates with one's success. Shape your attitude by steeping yourself in the most positive messages possible; at least you can allow yourself to win in your own mind!

Have you seen the movie *Apollo 13*? If you have, you may recall the phrase that was said at the turning point: "Failure is not an option." Gene Krantz, who was the commander in charge of Apollo 13, was standing at an easel pad. He had drawn two circles, one to represent the moon and the second the Earth. His people had told him that they could bring the spacecraft with the men only about 80% of the distance between the moon and the earth. He listened to all the problems: they had lost power and oxygen; the spacecraft had been damaged and they did not know if it would survive reentry into the Earth's atmosphere; carbon dioxide was building up in the module since it was built for two men and not three; the excessive carbon dioxide was impairing the astronauts' mental abilities; they only had one booster rocket to shoot off to get them on the right trajectory or they would miss the Earth. Very dire reports. Krantz had given the President of the United States five-to-one odds that the astronauts would **not** make it back.

Yet despite all of this "evidence," Gene drew a line from the 80% mark to the Earth and barked, "I want you to get them from there (the 80% mark) to here (the Earth) with time to spare. No American has been lost in space and none is going to be lost on my watch. Failure is not an option." He threw down the magic marker and walked out of the room.

What happened?

Magic! Anyone who had anything to do with the design, manufacturing, building, or fueling of the rocket was called in, and they worked around the clock. No one slept. Why did they do this? They should have given up, since what Gene wanted them to do was, for all intents and purposes, impossible. There were five-to-one odds against bringing the astronauts back. Why didn't they pack up and go home?

I believe it was because Gene had a passionate vision that, no matter what, these men were coming back. Did he have the answer and was not telling them? I do not think so. Was his ego out of control? I do not think so. I think he believed that the astronauts would come back. Period. I believe that if he allowed any doubt to creep into his mind, those men would not have returned. It would have been too easy for anyone to grab onto this doubt and run with it. Gene's tenacious insistence on the "impossible" brought those men home. Thank you, Gene!

The astronauts returned on twelve amps of power. That is less than it takes to run your vacuum cleaner. They did the impossible. It was not in their possible world, so they needed to invent a way that would work. It was not easy, not obvious. So if I were to ask you to double the amount of work you complete in a day and do it in one-half the time, you may respond that that is impossible. I understand that doing this is not within your possible world, but that does not mean it is impossible. You may have to stre-e-e-e-tch and be uncomfortable for awhile, but what if you found a way? Wouldn't you be proud of and pleased with yourself? Pretty exciting, huh?

The big paradigm-shifting question is "What is impossible to do today, but if you could do it would fundamentally change your business?"

Maintain an open mind. One of my favorite quotes is, "Minds are like parachutes: they only work when they are open." An open and curious mind will bring you untold joy, as well as solutions to many challenges in your life.

Watch your thoughts and expectations. In life, more frequently than not, we get what we expect. Actively seek other people's perspectives, since we all have blind spots that limit us from achieving our goals. My friend Carol is a venture capitalist in the entertainment industry. Carol joined her current firm ten years ago. She has brought in 26 times more revenue than any of the other partners. I asked her how she makes decisions. Her response was fascinating. She said that before she makes any decision she always asks two people: a woman who has been a homemaker, and Carol's young niece. I asked why. She said, "They are batting 1.000 with me. They do not understand the MBA language so I need to speak to them in terms they understand. But they have pointed out issues and concerns that I totally missed or did not think were important." So here is a woman who makes multi-million dollar decisions, and not only respects, but also follows the opinion of her niece and of a woman homemaker. Carol misses few business opportunities because she is willing to seek other people's perspectives, especially the perceptions of those that most people would ignore, assuming, "They cannot help me, because they do not understand my business." Please ask people outside your industry, as well as neighbors, friends and relatives. They will have opinions, and in their opinions you will discover nuggets of gold.

Summary

Make friends with change. When we do something new, our bodies (which yearn to feel comfortable) give us a shot of adrenaline in case we need to "fight or flee." Since oxygen burns off adrenaline, we must make it a daily practice to take lots of deep breaths.

Be willing to be uncomfortable because that is how you grow. Be willing to "fall on your diaper" a number of times when you are doing something new.

Take the lid off your expectations, and shoot for the moon. Most people aim too low and stop themselves from reaching their potential.

Shortly after his election in 1960, JFK said we would put a man on the moon in a decade, yet at that time we could not create a rocket that would successfully orbit the earth. They were crashing and burning, not launching. Wouldn't it have been more reasonable for him to say we will have a rocket successfully orbit the earth? It would have been safer, a lower risk. But what is important is to set goals high, because if we do not, we will definitely not reach them. We may not achieve a high goal but we surely will not reach it if we do not set our sights on it. Let it be our North Star, our dream, and aim high—very, very high.

In these chapters, we have laid the foundation for customer retention. It is an outside-the-box profit strategy whose potency is just beginning to be understood.

The Stunning Economics of Customer Retention

There are four core concepts of Customer Retention:

1. The powerful economics of customer retention
2. Market and customer segmentation
3. Viewing high operating costs as a symptom of low customer retention rates
4. The four stages of a customer relationship

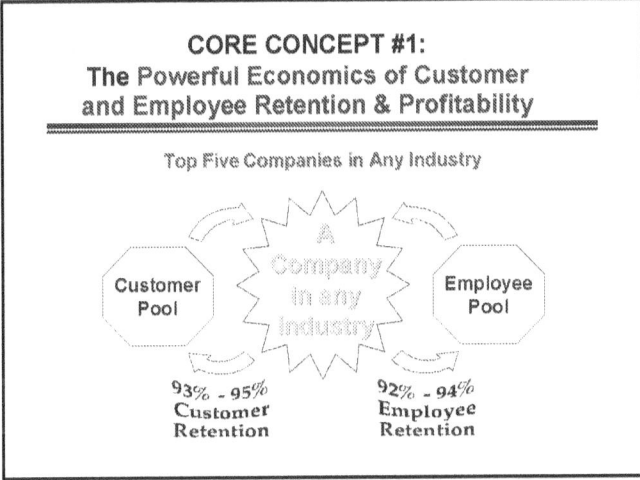

Very powerful economics underlie customer and employee retention. More and more companies are dedicating resources to keeping customers and employees, since it is very costly to replace them. The top five companies in any industry—you pick the industry—have a 93% to 95% retention rate. Most companies average around 78% to 82%. That is only the average. What does this mean to the typical company? Each year twenty percent of its customers leave. That means that the following year, if the company is to grow, the sales force needs to replace that twenty percent and add an additional five to ten percent. That means the company needs 25% to 30% new customers each year. That is an enormous strain on any company, its systems, its people and its resources. It is an ineffective and very costly way to grow a company. This expensive revolving door is not easily identified on the financials and thus can remain elusive. You must retain your most profitable customers, because replacing them is too expensive. Stop the leaky customer bucket! Companies need to know the cost of this problem in order to perform a cost-benefit analysis and decide whether undertaking a customer retention initiative will produce the expected financial results.

For example, consider the case of one of my clients, a company that ran a hotel. The hotel's telephone system was quirky. Sometimes at this hotel, a guest or a potential guest would call and would hear twenty or more rings before the call would be answered, although the phone in the hotel might ring only once or twice. Management wanted to know whether improving its telephone system, which would cost about $500,000, would be important to its best customers, and positively impact its bottom line. Survey results showed that 5% of the hotel's customers would leave within two years if the company did not fix the telephone system. Each client had a lifetime value of $375,000 and the 5% represented fifteen customers. It was a no-brainer to spend $500,000 to retain $5,625,000 of revenue!

Customer and employee retention strategies give companies powerful alternative routes to increasing profitability. Employee retention usually trails customer retention by two to three percentage points. The most valuable assets of any company wear shoes: the employees and customers. Employees are also internal customers, so everyone in every company serves many customers: some internal and some external. Who are your customers?

Leo Burnett, a large advertising firm based in Chicago, has maintained a client and employee retention rate of 98.5% or better for over twenty years! This is astonishing. For twenty years, the agency won every client it wanted, and its employees were fiercely dedicated to its success. These high retention numbers are possible to achieve! However, sustaining them is not easily accomplished.

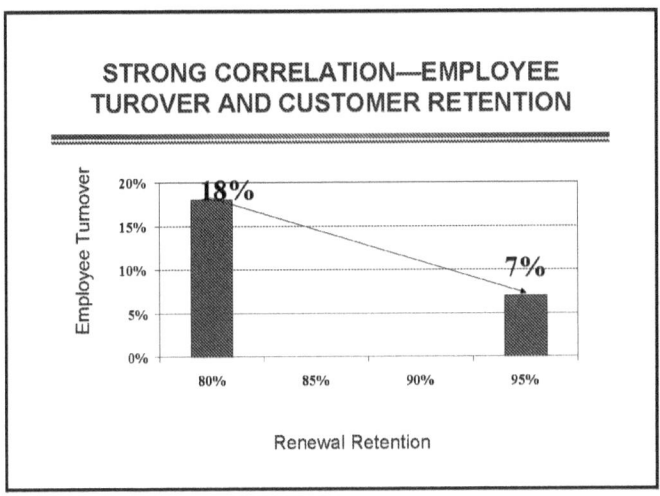

The relationship between employee and customer retention is well known but not well understood. From a Tillinghouse study in the insurance industry, companies with 7% employee turnover had a 95% customer retention rate, whereas with an 18% turnover, the retention rate was 80%. For an employee to be considered truly retained, s/he needed to have been offered another job for 10% to 15% more compensation and turned it down. Many people feel trapped in a job or have few viable options in the geographic area and thus are not truly loyal or retained. In fact, a Walker's Survey in 2001 revealed the following:

1. Only 24% of employees are truly loyal.
2. One out of three are halfway out the door.
3. The average employee's tenure is 3.4 years, and this number has been dropping in every industry except government.
4. About one-third of employees feel trapped.

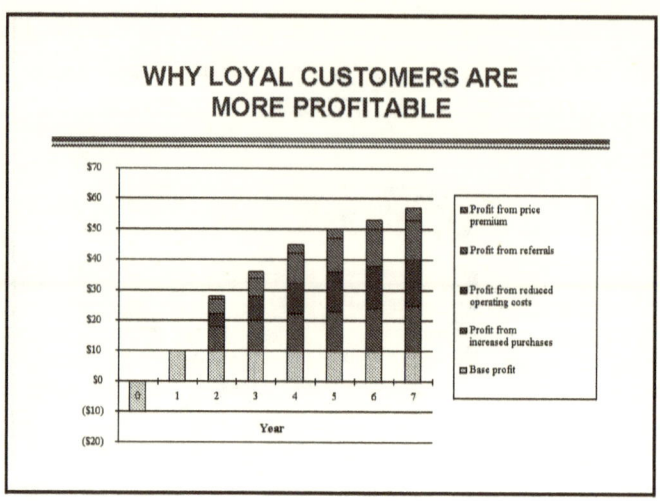

This graph of credit card company retention shows that the longer customers are with a company, the more profitable those customers are likely to become. The typical credit card company's customer acquisition costs are $10 to $50. The company recoups its acquisition costs in the first year. How long does it take your company to recoup its customer acquisition costs? For most companies, it takes two to five years. Then profit increases over time through customers' additional purchases, customers' referrals, lower operating costs and price premiums. Moreover, the longer customers are with a company, the less price-sensitive they tend to become. So if a customer leaves your business after two years or eight years, the one with eight years of tenure will most likely be taking a lot more profit. It is prudent to know how long former customers were with your company in order to correctly analyze how much profit your company loses with each customer defection.

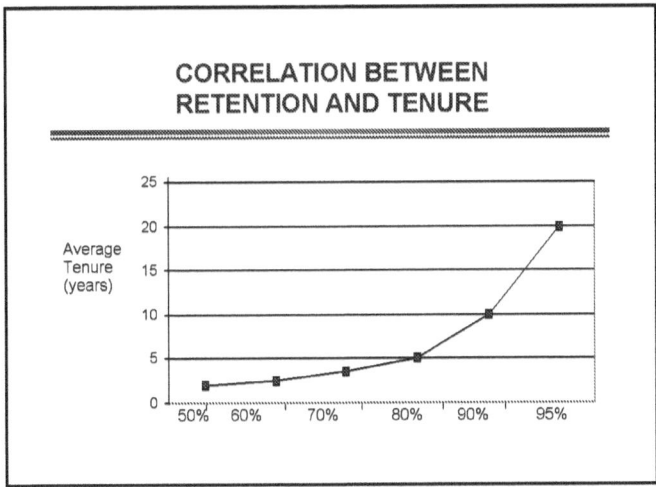

This shows the strong positive correlation of retention and tenure in another format. Somewhere before the fourth year and the seventh year, customers in all businesses become more loyal. The graph demonstrates this with the increased slope of the line. Thus it is economically prudent to reward employees for keeping customers past these "hump" years.

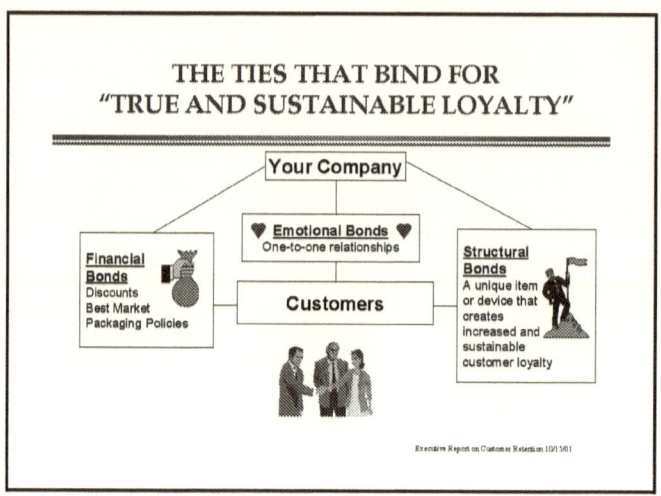

There are three different strategies that create loyalty, which in turn creates high retention: financial bonds, emotional bonds, and structural bonds. Financial bonds can be discounts, best markets and package pricing. Emotional bonds include customizing relationships with each customer and relationships that are built around the customer's needs. Structural bonds are the newest addition to strengthening loyalty with customers. A great example of a structural bond is Mobil's Speed Pass; as a customer, you only need to hold it up to the gas pump and a scanner will approve your purchase. No credit card, no person, no paper—just this one-and-a-half inch long, lightweight device that fits neatly on a key chain. Now that is a Wow! and forms a powerful structural bond.

When you are evaluating how your company creates loyalty, make sure you are striving to have a component in each of these areas.

Some companies decide to offer service standards or a guarantee to their customers to increase the value they offer. What can your company do to increase its value to your customers? See Appendices 23, 24, 25 and 26 for ideas and examples.

Not All Customers Are Equal—Market and Customer Segmentation

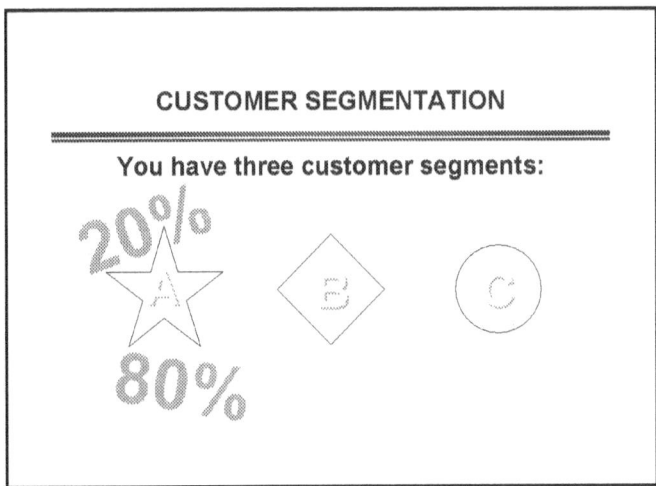

CUSTOMER SEGMENTATION

You have three customer segments:

20%
A
80%
B
C

The second Core Concept of Customer Retention is the necessity to segment a company's markets, as well as its customers. For some industries, this is automatic. Colleges select whom they want to accept, as do credit card companies and mortgage companies. Banks assess fees to the customers that are not profitable to them. These customers either pay the fees or leave the bank.

The airline industry was one of the first to segment its services, with first class, business class and coach. So when I travel, and I pass the people in first class while schlepping my hand luggage to coach, and see the first class passengers sitting in wide leather seats with a drink in their hand, I do not say, "It is not fair!" If I want the same treatment, the rules have been laid out: by spending two to three times more than the cost of a coach seat, I could be in first class, too.

Many industries have not laid out guidelines for different levels of service, and thus treat all customers more or less equally. Employees will be stressed and drained all the time, since it is impossible to treat everyone equally with a large customer base. Companies need to decide which customers are worth the investment of time and money it takes to create life-long bonds, and then create those bonds with these customers.

Many industries have not segmented their customer base, because up until now, economics did not demand that they do so to remain profitable. These companies have had healthy profit margins, so the "excess" service given to their least profitable customers was not a financial concern. As the economics have changed and these industries are challenged to have healthy profit margins each year, many of them are turning to segmentation to identify their most profitable customers. Many of these companies are still clinging to a dearly held yet antiquated belief: all customers are equal and thus they should all be treated equally. The updated version is a bit different: all customers deserve to be treated well, and some deserve extra time and effort. Most companies do not initially react positively to the idea of segmenting their customers. However, segmentation is a necessary prerequisite to retention and profits, as the article in Appendix 27 explains. Also in Appendix 27 contains some additional information on the 80/20 Rule. Appendix 28 explains the pitfalls and advantages of tiered service.

The best example of a company that segmented it market and has 25% higher profit margins because of this segmentation is Honda. A friend owns a number of car dealerships throughout the country. He said that his Honda dealerships are 25% more profitable than any of his other dealerships. Twenty-five percent is huge. Honda focused its marketing on the Baby Boomers, and through market research, learned what this generation wants in their cars.

Honda picked a large market and has done lifetime marketing. The company is "growing up" with the Baby Boomers. It started with the Civic and then the Accord, and then created the Accord wagon when the Boomers started to have children. Now the company has moved onto the luxury Sedans and SUVs. As the Boomers age, perhaps Honda will develop a car that will respond to the driver's voice, making it easy to adjust the seat for aging Boomers' aching backs or arthritic hips. By knowing its market well, Honda has created a line of automobiles that caters to its customers' needs and desires.

At a Honda dealership, each person who walks through the door is, in essence, a carbon copy of the person who just left. The easiest and most profitable way to sell is to have fundamentally one type of customer.

In contrast, consider my friend's GM dealerships. He says, "the salespeople have to sell a luxury car, a truck, a van, a sports car, a family car…. It is much easier to sell to one type of customer than to five or more types of customers." The lesson is to pick your one or two best types of customers, really understand their needs through market research, and give them what they want. If you can do this in a smooth and easy process, with surprises and delights, and create a compelling experience, you, too, can enjoy much higher levels of profitability. Conduct market research and then execute the initiatives to produce a healthy bottom line.

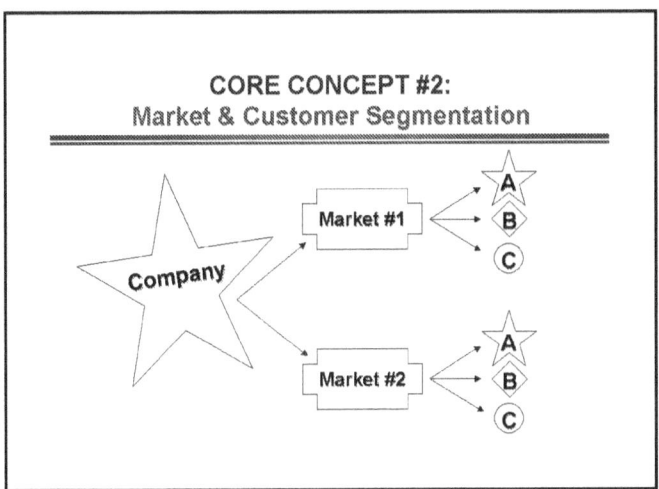

The fundamental purpose of segmentation is to recognize that customers have different needs, and thus they do not all need the same level of service. At the Bank of Boston, we segmented our customers into three categories: the Private Banking Group, the Zenith Group and the Retail group. In the Private Banking Group, the focus was on people who had relatively sophisticated investment needs: investing internationally, into commodities, precious metals, etc. These people needed to discuss a wide variety of sound investment options for their portfolios. The needs of the people in the Zenith Group were different. They were interested in Home Equity loans, retirement plans, mortgages, investing for a child's education and the like. Finally, the Retail section was for the remainder of the bank's customers, who would typically want a checking and saving account, an auto loan and a credit card.

The bank had clear guidelines for classifying customers as a Retail, Zenith or Private Banking Client. Customers had a positive experience, working with people who knew and understood their needs, and who were, in fact, experts at meeting their needs. A private Banker is of little use to a Retail client and a Retail banker is of little use to a Zenith client. Companies need to focus more on matching their employees' talents and skills with their clients' needs.

CUSTOMER SEGMENTS

What's wrong with this picture?

Customers	% of Base	% of Gross Revenue	% of Time Spent Acquiring & Retaining
☆	20%	80%	20%
B	30%	15%	30%
C	50%	5%	50%

What is wrong with this picture? The "A"s are the 20% of customers that produce roughly 80% of a company's profit. Since most companies treat all customers equally, companies spend approximately 20% of their time with the "A"s. The "B"s are the 30% of the customer base that generate 15% of the profit and take up about 30% of the company's time. The "C"s are the approximately 50% of the customer base that produce only 5% of a company's profit, but companies spend about 50% of their time working with them. If you wanted to increase this typical company's profitability, what are some possible strategies to implement?

First, you may want to spend more time with the "A"s. I recommend that a company spend at least 50% of its time on its "A" customers. These "A"s are generating 80% of the company's revenue; they are why the company is in business. Second, ask your current "A" customers for referrals of their friends, family and colleagues, who are most likely to also be "A"s. Third, I recommend finding a more cost-effective way to work with the "C"s if the company can devise a profitable operational strategy. Some companies have these "C" customers call only into automated systems.

A fourth strategy is to reduce the number of "C"s, or simply eliminate them. Many of you are saying, "These people are our bread and butter." No, it may seem that way, but since they produce only 5% of your company's revenue, they are actually taking away precious time that would be much more wisely spent with the "A"s. Most employees are very comfortable with the "C"s, since employees spend half of their day working with them. However, by reducing their numbers or eliminating them, you would only lose 5% of your revenue, but recover 50% of your time! Be forewarned that employees will be more uncomfortable working with the "B"s and "A"s, since employees have spent most of their time with the "C"s. The "B"s and the "A"s have different needs and wants, and initially, they may be more challenging for your employees to Wow!, but they are well worth the effort.

Yet it is the time you spend with the "C"s that is taking time away from the "A"s. If a dollar is supposed to buy a dollar's worth of service, who is not getting their money's worth? Who is receiving more than their share of service? Who is subsidizing whom? The truth is that the "A"s are subsidizing the "B"s and "C"s. If you were to be really honest, you would tell your "A" clients, "You fit with our company so well that you need less of our time. Because the "B"s and "C"s do not fit as well, need a lot of our time, and cannot afford to pay more, we cannot reduce your payments to reflect the time we spend with you."

A fifth strategy is to upsell to some of your customers. Once you objectively define your company's "A," "B" and "C" customers, you can then identify which "B" and "C" customers could become "A" and "B" customers, respectively.

Your ultimate goal is to duplicate and replicate the "A"s and eliminate the "C"s. A company needs to focus it resources on the precious few ("A"s) rather than the mediocre many ("C"s). A key sales method to replicate the "A"s is to ask your current "A"s for referrals. Since we tend to spend time with people like ourselves, "A"s will know mostly "A"s, "B"s know mostly "B"s and "C"s know mostly "C"s. Do **not** ask "C"s for referrals; you already have plenty!

Customer base segmentation is a critical step toward having high retention rates. Without it, a company cannot adequately distinguish itself to its customers to keep them for life. Without the goal of creating a compelling buying experience, complete with surprise and delight, for their most profitable customers, companies rarely will become consistently better than average in their industry.

Here is an example of how segmentation can assist employees to focus more of their time and attention on the "A"s. A simple change in office procedures will ensure that the "A"s receive the best service a company can offer. (For an example of specific guidelines for standards of service in office procedures, see Appendix 29.)

Example of Service Standards

Service Standards	Customers:		
	A	B	C
The reference to the number of days or hours is business days or hours			
1 # Hours For a Phone Call to Be Returned	4	8	24
2 # Hours Written Correspondence Will Be Acknowledged	8	16	32
3 # Days Claims Will Be Submitted to Insurance Company	1	1	1
4 # Days Certificates Will Be Mailed	1	2	3
5 Minimum # Contacts With Producer on Account During Policy Term	2	1	0
6 Special Pay Plans for Customers	Yes	No	No

Since your "A" customers generate 80% of your profits, they deserve the very best service your company can deliver. Many clients have devised internal standards of service for the three types of customers, and utilize these in their sales presentations with great success. However, a word of warning: before you promote these new standards, you must be absolutely sure that your company can deliver what it is promising. Keep in mind the adage, "underpromise and overperform." As a company continues to improve, its standards can be raised.

I remember one customer I surveyed, who said, "Many companies promise good service, but this company puts it in writing." That was the reason this person selected my client. My client stood out from the pack by defining the good service that this new "A" client would receive, rather than just promising to deliver this nebulous intangible called "good service" like all of his competitors. Appendix 30 provides a good example of one company's standards of performance "put in writing," in a format designed to be given to customers.

There are hundreds of ways a company can utilize segmentation to ensure that customers receive customized services that Wow! and delight them. See Appendix 31.

Many people are not aware of how market research can assist them to be more effective at their jobs. For instance, who are your best, most profitable customers? It is imperative to know who they are in order to uncover how to attract more of them. What objective criteria would you use to pinpoint them? Here is an example of segmentation criteria for "A," "B" and "C" customers.

"A" Clients

1.   Have been with the company a minimum of five years, AND

2. Use a minimum of three services with us, AND
3. Pay a minimum annual service charge of $50,000, AND
4. Have made payments on time for the past three years.

"B" Clients

1. Have been with the company a minimum of two years, AND
2. Use a minimum of two services with us, AND
3. Pay a minimum annual service charge of $25,000, AND
4. Have made payments on time for the past two years.

"C" Clients

1. Use a minimum of one service with us, OR
2. Pay a minimum annual service charge of $5,000.

As you see, a customer needs to meet all four criteria to be an "A" or "B" client, while a "C" client only needs to meet one of the criteria. Since 50% of a company's customer base are "C"s, it is easier for any company to attract more "C"s than "A"s or "B"s. See Appendix 32 to assess how successful you are at increasing the value of your customer base.

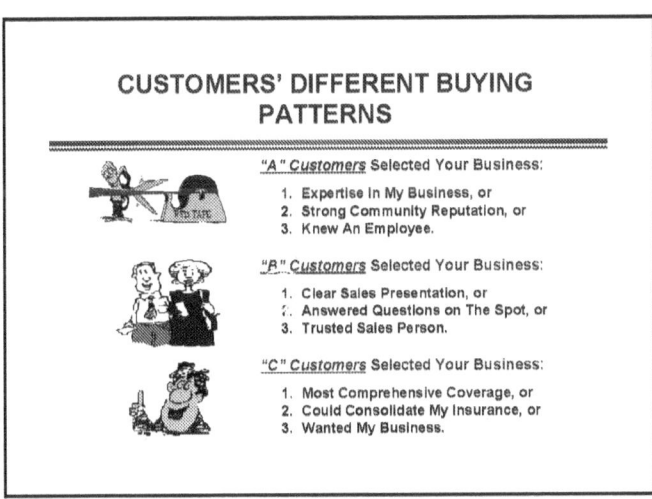

This is a hypothetical example of how knowing the reasons that your "A," "B" and "C" customers initially decided to do business with your company can assist salespeople in attracting more "A"s by using these reasons as screening questions. For instance, if you are with a prospect and want to know if this person will become an "A," ask him or her the three questions under "A"s. If you do not receive a nod or a yes to any of these, then you know with a 95% confidence level that that prospect will not become an "A." That will allow you to allocate your precious prospecting time elsewhere to produce the most profitable customers for your company. This is invaluable information for salespeople to be the most effective at their jobs.

Food for Thought

1. Your "A" clients are the source of your company's future growth.
2. The incessant need for new business and service requires so much time that it leaves an inadequate amount of time to "Wow!" existing "A" clients.
3. When "A" clients are lost, they tend to be replaced with "C" clients because "C"s are the most numerous and easiest to acquire.
4. Losing an "A" client has three to seven times the impact on profitability as losing a "C" client.
5. The most profitable clients are "A"s who renew and refer.

This illustrates the powerful advantages of utilizing referrals as the main source of new business. First, your "A" customers are the source of your company's future growth. If you look at who your company's "A" customers were five years ago and who your new ones are today, it's likely that 85% of the new ones came from the "A"s, through referrals, additional subsidiaries, or other means. Current "A" customers will fuel your company's future growth. Care for them well so they will produce a handsome return to you in the future.

Secondly, many people complain that they do not have time to Wow! their clients. If employees are not focusing on "A" clients, many employees will probably be complaining about never having enough time. This will be accurate, as a company cannot treat all customers superbly well; it is not possible. A company needs to develop a strategy to utilize its people and their time to maximize its profits. Have your "A" employees working with your "A" customers so the customers are receiving the best your company can offer.

Third, when an "A" customer is lost, salespeople tend to scramble and replace the customer with many "C"s, since they are the most numerous and the easiest to sell to. The disadvantage for the company is that even if the company makes the same income from fees or commissions, it now has five customers, and needs to set up five accounts, service them, and interact with them. Five new customers represent a highly significant additional financial and time burden on the company compared with that of one known customer.

Fourth, losing an "A" client has three to seven times the impact on profitability than does losing a "C." Not all customers are equal in terms of profitability. I have seen situations where losing an "A" customer had forty times as much impact on the bottom line as losing a "C" did.

Fifth, the most profitable customers are those that stay with you over time and refer people like themselves. Your job is to replicate and duplicate the "A"s!

The Hidden and Strangling Cost of Rework in Service Businesses

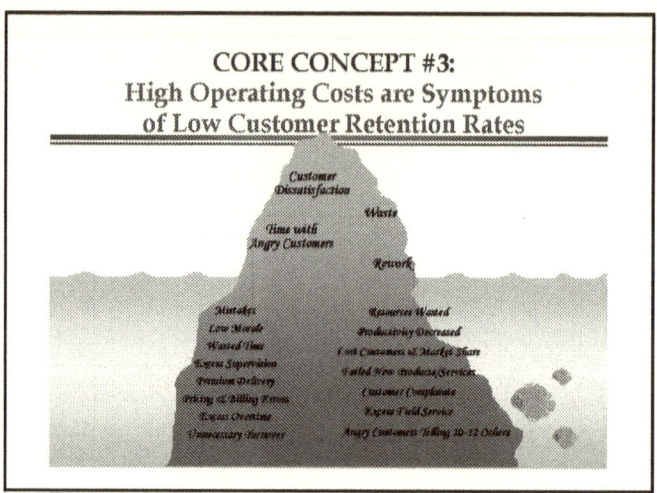

CORE CONCEPT #3:
High Operating Costs are Symptoms
of Low Customer Retention Rates

The third Core Concept of Customer Retention is that high costs are not a problem in and of themselves, but rather are a symptom of a low customer retention rate. With my accounting and tax background, I can probe underneath financials and identify the root cause that is producing the high expenses and/or low profits.

An example comes from a client with low sales hit ratios. The company wanted its salespeople to be more successful. By interviewing prospects who decided not to do business with the company, I discovered that the salespeople had a poor screening process. Most of these prospects were very loyal to their current agent (would not leave for less than a 25% price differential) and thus had no pain to resolve. Additionally, the agency's sales manager would not hire salespeople whom he perceived would be better than he was, and thus the overall quality of the salespeople was low. So, having started with low sales hit ratios as the problem, we identified two root causes: a poor screening process and an insecure sales manager who would not hire superior salespeople.

Low customer retention is usually a factor. A company that retains 93% to 95% of its most profitable customers will almost always generate a healthy profit. Rarely, some extraordinary expense occurs which leads to a one-time loss.

Most service businesses spend 30% to 50% of their budgets on re-doing work. The difference between service and manufacturing financials is that with the latter, there is a number on the financial statement that is called rework and thus can be managed. What is the equivalent on the service side? My bet is that Customer Service departments take that role. Rather than eliminate the root causes of problems, most companies fixate on symptoms and then create departments to resolve the same problem again and again for different customers. Few companies keep reliable complaint logs and then analyze the logs to identify the root causes of recurring problems. Fix the root cause and about ten to twenty symptoms will disappear!

The more paper-intensive an industry is, the higher the percentage of rework it will require. It is estimate that 85% of policies that leave an insurance company contain errors, while 58% of those that leave an agency contain errors. There is an outrageously high tolerance for errors in the insurance industry. Errors are the norm rather than the exception.

Some companies find it difficult to pinpoint rework, so I have provided some examples of rework that initially seem to be "acceptable" expenses. See Appendix 33.

Think of how many industries would not even be in business if 58% of what they produced contained errors. The medical profession is a great example. If doctors were to make errors in 58% of their cases, those doctors would be out of business. If pharmacies gave the wrong medication to patients 58% of the time, they would be out of business. How about the airline business? Fifty-eight percent of the flights would not take off, and of the ones that did, 58% would land at the wrong destinations. How about the banking or the telephone industries? Fifty-eight percent of the deposits and withdrawals on your banking statement would not be yours. Imagine the cheerful conversations you would have with the banking representative, who would reply, "Well, that is the way we do business." There would be no better choices because that would be the expected norm. I think we would all be unbearably frustrated if 58% of the telephone numbers we dialed did not reach the correct person. We would find alternative ways to communicate, because that number of incorrect connections would be intolerable.

The Four Distinct Stages of a Customer Relationship

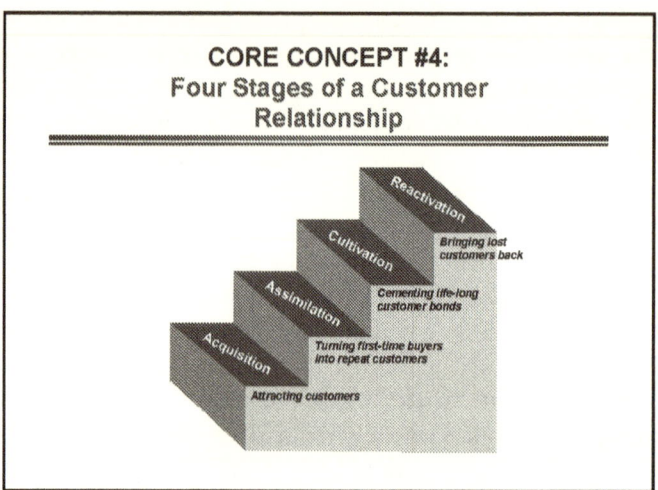

The fourth Core Concept of Customer Retention is that a customer relationship has four stages: acquisition, assimilation, cultivation and reactivation. Did you know that? Most people are not aware of these four distinct stages. Each company needs to pinpoint what each of its "A" and "B" customers need in each stage to be Wow!ed and delighted. Few companies even have the data to start analyzing; in essence, they are operating in the dark. Each of these stages will be discussed in detail in the next section.

Summary

In brief, these are the Four Core Concepts of Customer Retention:

- Customer retention is the driver of profitability. It usually produces a 15:1 ROI.
- To retain your most profitable customers, you must identify your distinct markets and then segment them. List each customer segment's need for each stage of a customer relationship.

- Reduce rework and do it now! It is sucking the life out of your people, weighing down processes, Whoa!ing your customers, and shrinking your profit margins!
- Be aware of the four stages of the customer relationship, and tailor your efforts to your customers' needs as they pass through each stage.

"Marketing and sales have been defined by some as the art of getting and keeping customers. Much of sales has been cast around the 'getting' problem. We have neglected the 'keeping' problem. Keeping requires some thought; it goes beyond what the customer service department does. It gets into how to satisfy the customer, how to get the customer to be a frequent buyer, and how to form links with customers, creating exit barriers that make it more expensive to leave than stay."[1]

To understand how to win, retain and win back customers, you need to understand in detail how to customize your approach to each client at each one of the four stages.

---

1 Planning Review Special Issue, Sept./Oct. 1992

Getting Customers for Life—The Acquisition Stage

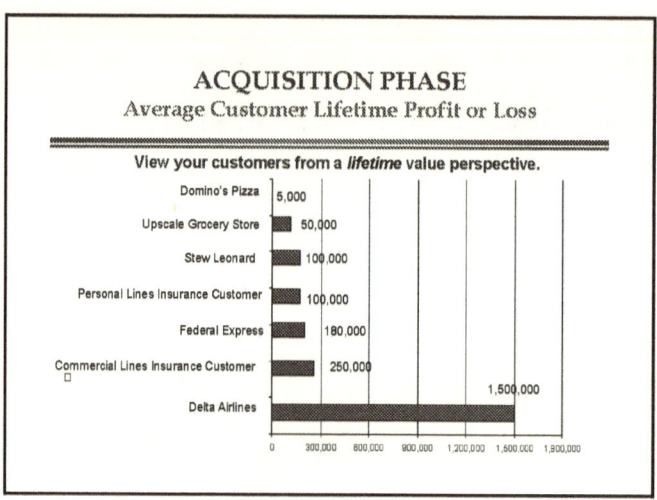

ACQUISITION PHASE
Average Customer Lifetime Profit or Loss

View your customers from a *lifetime* value perspective.

Domino's Pizza	5,000
Upscale Grocery Store	50,000
Stew Leonard	100,000
Personal Lines Insurance Customer	100,000
Federal Express	180,000
Commercial Lines Insurance Customer	250,000
Delta Airlines	1,500,000

It amazes me how many companies are so focused on new business that they allow existing business, the business that they have already invested time and money in, to just walk out the door. Companies have made a significant investment to acquire their customers and the trust of those customers. It is necessary for companies to spend money to protect their investment. By doing so, the company is protecting the customer revenue stream that they have earned. Be willing to spend a small amount to protect your larger and more lucrative investment.

Some companies only look at this year's revenue or profit to assess the value of a customer. I strongly advocate adopting a longer-term perspective: what is each customer's lifetime value to your company? Another way to say it is, what is the present value of each customer's lifetime revenue stream? For example, if a customer generates $2,000 annual profit and the average lifetime of a customer in your company's business is ten years, a more accurate perspective is that that customer represents $20,000. If then you add in cross-selling opportunities, referrals and a decrease in operating expenses associated with continuing, a typical $20,000 lifetime value customer can be easily worth over $50,000. Your company may decide that it wants to interact with and service a customer worth $50,000 quite differently than it would do with one worth $2,000.

It is vital for a company to calculate the lifetime revenue stream that each current and potential customer represents. Why? This will allow a company to make informed and economically wise decisions. Without this information, how does a company know for sure if it would be worthwhile to invest in upgrading its computer systems? Will an upgrade increase its customer retention, and thus its profitability?

By nature, customers are loyal. None of us wants to leave any company we are currently working with. In fact, we hope and some pray that nothing will go wrong, since we have precious little free time to spend locating another company. Yet, each year most companies "chase" 20% of their customers out their doors and to their competitors, and with those customers goes not just the current year's profit, but their entire lifetime revenue stream. Ouch!

Viewing customers from the lifetime point of view also allows companies to take a fresh look at their employees. What is the value of the book of business an employee handles? Does the person even know what his/her book of business is worth? How well trained is that person in retaining each customer and each customer's lifetime revenue stream? Is that person rewarded when s/he does a superb job at keeping a customer? See Appendices 34 and 35 to find out how well you understand the economics of customer retention and the relationship between retention and profitability.

To have an idea of what your business or book of business is worth, do some simple calculations. How much revenue does your average customer generate in a year? What is your gross profit? On average, how many years does a customer stay with your business? Multiply the number of years a customer is expected to stay by your gross profit per customer, and you will understand the value of **one** new customer. This can be eye opening!

The four industries with the highest customer acquisition costs are:

1. Insurance
2. Banking
3. Automobile sales
4. Hotel and travel

These are the industries that invest the most to obtain a new customer, and thus have the greatest potential to improve by focusing on retention. They also have the greatest risk, because when a customer leaves, the company needs to incur high customer acquisition costs to replace that customer. This not only takes a financial toll on the company, but also takes an emotional toll on employees.

The insurance industry's cost to replace a customer is eleven to thirteen times higher than its cost to retain a current customer. Most companies are too focused on the front door: new customers. A prudent economic decision is to invest some financial and human resources in retaining customers. It has an average 15:1 ROI. Where does your company focus its resources? Is there another activity your company is undertaking that produces a 15:1 ROI? There is none.

The Power of Perseverance

It is imperative for salespeople to be prepared to hear, on average, four "No"s from a prospect before hearing a "Yes." Why? Usually, prospects' "No"s are objections that have not been clarified or responded to. If the salesperson keeps returning to profitable prospects at opportune times, eventually the salesperson will most likely obtain their business. Be willing to hear many "No"s, or you will be missing many sales by moving on too quickly to the next prospect.

44% of salespeople give up after one "No"
22% of salespeople give up after two "No"s
14% of salespeople give up after three "No"s
12% of salespeople give up after four "No"s

That leaves only 8% of all salespeople who will ask for a prospect's business more than four times. Thus, 8% of the salespeople are getting 60% of the business by being determined enough to keep asking! Salespeople must be persistent and friendly.

ACQUISITION PHASE
Where Does Your Business Spend Most of
Its Time, Effort, and Resources?

For a Single Sale	You Must Contact	At a Cost of
New Customers	20 People	$2,673
Former Customers	10 People	$ 625
Referred Customers	6 People	$ 903
Existing Customers	4 People	$ 280

The figures above represent customer acquisition costs for the insurance industry and include the average costs for five different agencies.

- One out of twenty prospects who have never heard of your company will become a customer. This is the hardest sale because there is no pre-existing bond of trust.
- One out of ten former customers will return if asked. With a former customer, the bond was broken, and it is usually easier to mend a broken bond than to create a new one.
- One out of six referred customers will become a customer.
- One out of four existing customer will purchase additional services and products.

So where does your company focus its time, efforts and resources? Most companies spend the vast majority of their time and resources on new customers, customers who have the lowest sales-hit ratio and thus are the most expensive customers to acquire. This is not economically sound, but it is what people have been doing for years and it worked well enough up until now. It has been the most prudent method to keep profits high. In these challenging times, a new strategy is called for. Salespeople should not spend so much of their time and energy seeking new customers; in fact, this approach is economically imprudent.

In today's marketplace, as profit margins are being sliced, companies need to find better methods to attract profitable customers. Profitability and growth comes from three primary strategies: cross-selling, asking for referrals and asking former customers to return. A simple way to work cross-selling into your sales presentation is to ask, toward the end, "By the way, do you have _____(product or service)?" This is a smooth and effective way to increase business with individual customers. After you have cross-sold your current customers, ask these customers for referrals.

Salespeople rarely ask former profitable customers to come back. Most salespeople prefer to seek new business, even with its lower sales hit ratios, retention rates, etc. It is imperative for all salespeople to feel comfortable staying in touch with former customers, and when appropriate, to ask them to return.

These three activities will produce lower expenses, higher profit margins, and happier customers and salespeople. However, old habits can be hard to break; thus, many companies need to motivate employees to break those habits by reexamining their compensation structures and making sure they are appropriately rewarding the salespeople who focus their efforts in these more profitable areas.

The Retention Force of Cross-selling and Referrals

This cartoon illustrates how uncomfortable it can be for many people to start cross-selling. They may need to learn how to sell different products and services.

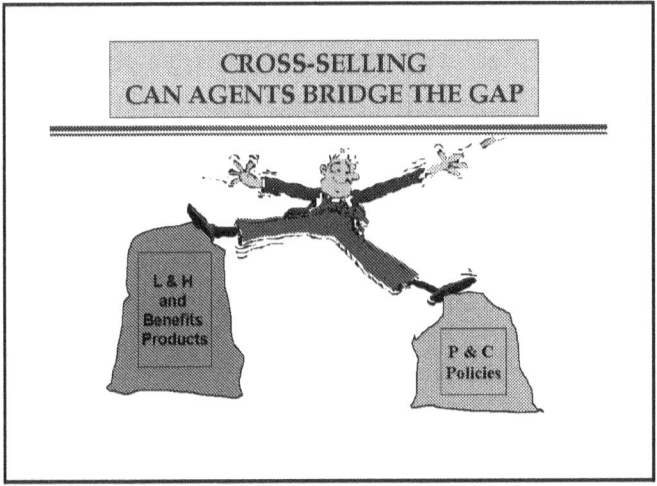

Traditionally, salespeople do not focus enough attention on cross-selling. As we discussed above, cross-selling is the easiest and most profitable method to add new business. An additional benefit is that it increases retention. There are classic barriers to retention when a salesperson "owns" the customers. Some examples are "The client is too busy." "The account is just fine, and I do not want to take a chance that we will make a mistake on other products and jeopardize the business I have." These fears need to be put aside so cross-selling can be a maximized, since it is key retention tool that absolutely must be utilized for the benefit of the company, and thus for everyone!

Salespeople may need to trust another employee or department with "their" customers. For many people, this represents new territory and thus is uncomfortable. The good news is that with practice, people will become comfortable with this change. See Appendix 36 for an effective letter to send to a prospect obtained through a referral in order to set up a meeting.

Since obtaining referrals is everyone's job, it is imperative that people in a company feel comfortable asking for referrals. The only way to feel comfortable with something that is new is to practice it many times until it is second nature. Salespeople need to practice in front of a mirror, with a colleague, in the car, in the shower, to your spouse, in front of a video camera…

When you are speaking, either in person or on the telephone, with a customer who is happy with what you have done for him/her, this is the perfect opening to ask for a referral. Say, "I am delighted that you are happy with my service. I enjoy making customers like you happy. Do you have any friends, colleagues or neighbors who you think would like to have similar great service?" Then wait. If s/he says "No," thank the person and move on. If there is some hesitation, ask what is that about. Care enough to assist them in giving you a referral. If they say, "I do not give referrals," thank the person and move on. Most people enjoy referring friends to companies that they have outstanding relationships with.

I have interviewed hundreds of my clients' customers. I regularly ask the question, "How could Company X find five more clients just like you?" Approximately one-third will respond, "If they ask me, I will tell them!" So ask them, today and every day!

Referrals are the main method that many companies use to obtain new business. In some industries, few people ever ask for referrals; this makes finding new customers more difficult and expensive.

There are numerous economic bonuses for asking for referrals. Some examples:

1. A referred "A" customer will, on average, give you three to five times more business than will a non-referred "A" customer.
2. Referred customers have the lowest acquisition costs.
3. Referred customers have the highest sales hit ratios.
4. "A" customers have a 25% higher retention rate over the first two to three years than customers obtained through any other marketing method.

For an example of a Cross-selling Bonus Plan see Appendix 37.

Why would anyone attempt to obtain new business except through referrals? Economically, it is far superior to any other method and produces bottom line results very rapidly. It is only the power of our old habits that keep us from excelling!

Learning the Smart Way—Debriefing

8th draft
1:15 a.m. Still not good enough.
Never settle.

In many industries, practice is part of the way the business is conducted. Think of sports. When a baseball player makes the major leagues, s/he does not sit back and say, "I do not need to practice now that I have made the Big Time." In fact, s/he probably practices more than ever. The same is true for the arts. When musicians have been accepted into the New York Philharmonic, they do not rest on their laurels and think "I do not need to practice any more; I have arrived!"

Yet in many industries, salespeople do not rehearse their sales presentations prior to the moment they stand in front of their prospective clients. This is a high-risk way to make a presentation. Do low-risk rehearsals and your sales effectiveness will skyrocket!

When I was at Bank of Boston Private Bank and Arthur Andersen & Co., I rehearsed my sales presentations not once, twice, three, four or five times, but a minimum of six times, to my colleagues and superiors. They would pull my presentation apart and I would put it back together, and then they would pull it apart again and I would put it back together again. By the time I was in front of the client, I was in perfect form. There was not a question that the client could ask, nor an objection the client could raise, that I had not already handled in my rehearsals. We did not keep track of our sale-hit ratios; we just obtained the customers we wanted, because we focused our efforts on the vital few and got them!

Another way to improve sales efforts is to debrief after sales presentations. Technology companies find this very effective. Most salespeople think they know why a prospect decided to do or not do business with them. Very few **ask** the prospects.

A consulting firm wanted to increase its sales effectiveness. It decided to make an up-front agreement with a prospect that, if the consulting firm were to make a presentation, the prospect would agree to debrief. That is, after the prospect made his or her decision, s/he would be willing to be interviewed by a person from the consulting firm, who was not involved in the presentation, to uncover why that prospect decided as he or she did. After six months of this process, the consulting firm's sales hit ratio went from 58% to 96%. It became evident that there were only three to five important factors to sell to a prospect. Thus, the company's presentations became sharper, more effective and shorter. For some guidelines around debriefing meetings, see Appendix 38. For a form to use to foster testimonials, see Appendix 39.

Summary

- Look at customers from the point of view of their Lifetime Value.
- Use referrals to obtain new business.
- Cross-sell to existing customers to gain the largest share of their wallet.
- Ask former profitable customers to come back.
- Rehearse requests for referrals.
- Rehearse all sales presentations to your "A" and "B" prospects at least five times.
- Debrief after a sales presentation to learn why your prospect decided to do or not to do business with you.

In order for your company to be successful in differentiating itself from its competitors, it needs to create a Unique Selling Proposition. This is a succinct list of five compelling reasons a prospect should do business with your company. See Appendix 40 for an example. For a list of revenue-generating activities that a manger needs to follow, see Appendix 41.

Orienting Your New Customers—the Assimilation Stage

The assimilation stage, which is the amount of time it takes the average customer to be fully assimilated into a company, usually lasts two to three years. At this stage, a company's goal is to accelerate customers' loyalty, since for many companies, two to three years is too long to have a customer remain less than 100% committed to staying. It is also too long to wait to reap the benefits of the next stage, the Cultivation Phase.

There are various techniques to accelerate the loyalty process. The first one is to develop a "Welcome Aboard" Package. Most companies do not provide an orientation process to their customers, thus lumping in new customers with those who have been with a company for many years. The result is that the new customers, who have many questions that the company could have anticipated and proactively answered, but did not, usually will not have all their questions answered in a timely and accurate way. This causes confusion and misunderstandings, a less-than-ideal beginning. An example would be a new client's typical questions when receiving the first invoice. The company could proactively respond to the likelihood of new customers' confusion by including a mock-up of an invoice in advance, with items circled and identified by drawing a line to the margin with an explanation. Other common items our clients have included in their "Welcome Aboard" packages are: a listing of all their products and services, their web site address, their hours of operation, contact telephone numbers, a glossary of industry terms, and the like.

A second effective method to accelerate new customers' loyalty is to send handwritten "Thank You" notes. In this age of computerized form letters, a handwritten Thank You note is refreshing, and is noticed. A company could thank the customer for being so cooperative, patient, and organized, or thank the customer for a conversation. We recommend every employee send two handwritten Thank You notes every day to two "A" customers.

A third technique is to call a new customer approximately one week after s/he has become a customer and ask, "How is everything?" We can frequently learn how to improve what we do by watching how other industries address certain issues. The automobile industry has the third-highest customer acquisition costs, after the insurance and banking industries. Automobile dealers regularly call customers who purchased a new car one week later. The reason is that, although when a customer purchases an item, s/he is deemed 100% loyal, the customer's loyalty level will rise or decline depending on the number of positive or negative interactions s/he has with someone at the company. Each interaction either increases or decreases loyalty by 20%, depending on whether the customer perceives it as positive or negative. Thus, when the new car dealership calls the week after a new car purchase and asks, "How is everything?" the call serves to increase loyalty by 20%. The chances are small that something has gone wrong with a brand new car in one week, so the call serves to increase loyalty. This customer is now as loyal as he or she can get. Six months down the line, the dealer or manufacturer will send a survey, which will increase loyalty another 20%.

Although the automobile industry is doing many things right, it could still improve its customers' loyalty by customizing the proactive contact it makes with them. Some people are annoyed by a telephone call, and would rather have a letter, while for others, no contact is preferable. Auto dealers have a powerful concept, but it could be made even more effective by tailoring it to each customer.

Also, auto dealers could develop a New Customer Team, consisting of the employees who are best at explaining the basics to the new customer, and who do it with enthusiasm and delight. ADP has developed what it calls the First Year Team, which works with new customers of a certain size for their first year. The following year, these customers work with the Second Year Team, and finally, the Third Team, which is their Team for the duration of their tenure as customers. ADP has retained 97% of the clients it wants to keep and has experienced double-digit growth for over twenty years. The company has built into its infrastructure the recognition that customers' needs differ based on the number of years customers have been with the company.

Some companies assign each new customer an advocate within their company for the first year. This would be a different person than the one with whom the customer works on a regular basis. This gives the new customer an additional resource within the company to help get his/her needs met. Lastly, companies must make their web sites interactive. Use as few images as possible, since many people do not have a fast connection, and images slow down their access. Make web pages colorful, keep them simple, and offer an informative "Tip of the Month," which will keep customers returning each month to read your latest tip.

There are a number of checklists that you can utilize to make your web sites as friendly and easy to use as possible.

To encourage customers to visit your site frequently, to be twice as loyal and to buy twice as much, you can allow them to post messages, or provide product reviews.

Summary

- Be easy for customers to work with.
- Anticipate new customers' needs with a "Welcome Aboard" kit.
- Genuinely care about them, and ask them interactive questions to elicit their needs.
- Provide them with a customer advocate within your company, and also assign them to New Customer Team, to smooth out the wrinkles of being with your company for the first time.

Cementing Those Relationships for Life—Cultivation Phase

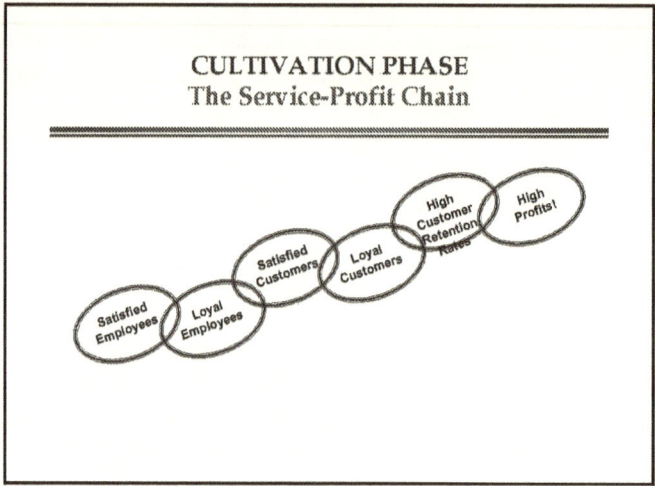

CULTIVATION PHASE
The Service-Profit Chain

The Service-Profit Chain is a powerful concept developed at Harvard Business School in 1992. It illustrates the relationships among customers and employees with loyalty, retention and profits. People have wondered, "Do I need loyal employees to create loyal customers who will produce high profits, or is it more important to provide great service which will generate loyalty and then the profits follow?" This Chain illustrates that any company must start with satisfied employees who become loyal employees. These employees create satisfied customers who become loyal customers. These loyal customers will stay, creating high levels of retention, and thus, high profits. Most companies want high profits, but they need to start at the beginning and examine how they are creating satisfied employees. Any chain is only as strong as its weakest link.

The top two ways to increase employee satisfaction and morale are: first, provide employees with interesting work, and second, appreciate them. Appreciation is so basic, and yet most companies frequently overlook it as a key strategic tool for increasing profits. Your company will not achieve sustainable long-term profitability unless your employees master giving and receiving appreciation. In this country, we are very good at giving criticism; every one of us can look at one page of typed material and immediately zoom in on the one or two errors. We are great at that, and it certainly has its place. However, we are not nearly as talented at zooming in on what an employee has done superbly and complimenting him/her. Companies that maintain at high levels of profitability for a sustained time period have **all** mastered the art of appreciating their employees. Appreciation does not cost anything but its value is incalculable. When employees feel appreciated, morale and productivity will multiply! Most employees are starved for appreciation, literally starved. Please give them genuine, caring, specific and immediate appreciation, and watch their productivity soar!

Dwight D. Eisenhower had a powerful message about how best to reward and recognize people. "Most people want to do a good job—as long as someone appreciates their efforts and encourages them. That's where good leaders put their greatest efforts—show people that their work is valuable and appreciated." His words are right on track with what I have found over the fourteen years I have been in the loyalty and retention business. Almost always, the top and most productive employees have bosses that regularly appreciate them. Many people have realized that the more they focus on what employees do well, the more of it their employees do. The bosses who were rated highest by their employees gave a five times as much positive feedback as negative.

Most of us are at the opposite end of the spectrum. As a society, we are so good at criticism and so ill equipped to catch people doing something great! Train yourself to be a detective searching for the best activity each of your employees has done today so you can compliment them on it. Many people have difficulty receiving compliments. I advise them to practice, practice and practice. Learn to give and receive compliments with grace and ease.

If you were to really implement this one technique of appreciating employees, this alone would have your employee retention—and thus, your profits—dramatically increase. Never underestimate the power of genuine appreciation. See Appendix 42 for an excellent article on affordable retention perks.

It is fascinating to look at the best companies to work for, and to see their striking similarities. Seventy-four percent of these companies have never had a mass layoff, and cite job security as a serious differentiator between them and other companies in their field.

Sixty percent offer formal mentoring programs; 59% offer flextime, while the other 41% consider it on a case-by-case basis. Fifty percent offer stock options to everyone; 33% offer on-site child care, home purchasing assistance and college planning assistance; 100% offer tuition reimbursement. How does your company compare? Where can your company improve, to attract and retain the best and the brightest employees for life?

Look at Appendix 43 to see how the work environment is changing to retain top talent. Protectiveness is being transformed into sharing. Lying and cover-ups are giving way to truth and openness. As companies shift from not risking to risking, morale and productivity will both increase dramatically.

High turnover rates are becoming lower turnover rates, as loyalty increases. No longer is a job a person's sole focus; increasingly, people seek more balance in their lives. Employer/employee hierarchy has become more like a partner-ship. Communication has shifted from "top down" to more interactive, as employers more frequently ask employees for feedback. New employees' on-the-job-training is being supplemented with continuous training throughout an employee's tenure.

These shifts portend a major shift in the work environments that will help companies to attract and retain the best, most talented people who can take a company to new heights.

Experts estimate that hiring and training a new employee will cost 50% to 60% of a departed employee's annual compensation. The average cost of losing an employee is $50,000.

In companies that are publicly traded, there is well-known positive correla-tion between employee morale and higher shareholder returns. Thus, creating and maintaining happy employees positively affects the bottom line. If we had access to privately held companies' financials, I am confident that we would see the same correlation. There is nothing unique about how publicly held compa-nies operate that would impact employees' decisions to stay with or leave a company differently from the way operations of privately held companies would.

There is a fascinating concept that pulls together much of what was just dis-cussed that is called the customer-employee mirror. According to this princi-ple, the way management and colleagues treat each other is an **exact** mirror of how employees will treat customers. It is very accurate, and becoming aware of employees' positive and negative patterns of communication is very powerful. For examples, see Appendices 44 and 45.

Over many years in this business, I have found that "Heart power is the strength of your organization." Will you tell the truth, whether "positive" or "negative"? Will you tell a colleague the s/he is causing problems by not meeting deadlines, or tell your boss that s/he is a terrific mentor, or tell the receptionist that s/he really needs to ask more questions since customers are regularly trans-ferred to the wrong person? Companies that really want the truth from their employees create highly empowered employees who excel. Because these com-panies care about their employees, employees' needs are being met, and the employees in turn can care about the customers. Genuine heartfelt caring is the passion that separates the mediocre from the extraordinary.

The glue that holds any company together is the strength of the relationships between the customers and employees. So both internal and external customers need to be Wow!ed. Wow!ing employees has two equally important components: the way employees treat one another creates 50% of the Wow! factor for the employees, while the way management treats employees comprises the other 50%. Thus, to Wow! employees, a company can start with the employees or the management, but it is vital that the company does indeed start.

THE BALANCE OF LIFE

◆ Supervisors rated by their employees as "family-responsive" retained employees twice as long

◆ John Hancock Financial Services says its family programs save the company about $500,000 a year in reduced turnover and absenteeism

Balance of Life has emerged as an important concept in the work place. Supervisors who are family-friendly retain employees twice as long as those who are not family-friendly. Retaining employees twice as long is impressive, indeed. It is crucial for companies to assist employees in finding the best balance for them between work and family. Some people would prefer more time off rather than a salary increase. Because of the fast pace of changes, a new generation occurs every five years. Thus, each employee needs to have some choice about the benefits s/he selects since all employees of any company are representatives of so many generations. Companies need to customize benefits for their top employees to ensure that they will remain fiercely loyal to the company for life.

Communication—The Essential Ingredient for Success

There are three basic levels of communication in an organization. The first is from Management to employees, the second is from employees to Management, and the third is from one employee to another. All three of these levels are vital to an organization, because they allow everyone to give and receive meaningful feedback. Feedback is a four-letter word, and the word is G-R-O-W! Without feedback, an employee could be off-course for a long time. That is not a strategy that will lead to high levels of productivity and profits.

The first level of communication is from Management to employees. Management needs to communicate to employees the company's direction and goals, and how their jobs fit into the picture. Additionally, Management needs to inform employees about how well they are doing, and Management needs to do this more frequently than once a year. Management should schedule at least two, and preferably four, reviews per year per employee, designed to accentuate the positive so employees can excel. I strongly also recommend 360 degree performance reviews, because many employees' performances are hindered by poor managers, and Management may not be aware of the problem.

The second level of communication is from employees to Management. Employees need to be realistic about what they can deliver and when. I strongly recommend following the adage, "Underpromise and overperform," when you are establishing a deadline for a deliverable. For example, an employee may have an important report to complete, and could only complete the report by the end of the week if everything goes without a hitch (which has not happened in years!). The wisest course for this employee would be to promise to complete it by the middle of the following week; if the employee completes the report sooner, s/he will be deemed a very productive employee. Most people do the opposite: they overpromise and underperform. This causes Management to lose confidence in employees, and employees to lose credibility with Management.

The third level of communication is from employees to other employees. What employees need from one another is more positive and caring feedback. Stop the bitching, complaining, backstabbing, gossiping, and triangulation, and stop it **now**! People's lives have been ruined by these childish and immature behaviors. My rule of thumb is that you have three business days to tell a person about the impact of his/her behavior, or drop it. I know many people who are dragging large trunk loads of unspoken resentments and anger from the past, which weigh on them and affect everyone they interact with. If you want things to improve, I recommend that you start by looking in the mirror and honestly assessing what you currently do that contributes—or does not contribute—to creating a Wow!ed work environment. Most people are doing much more to create a Whoa! work environment than a Wow! work environment. It is your choice, and a positive climate begins with you!

In the Appendix, I have included some examples of word choices that will improve relationships with colleagues, an article that discusses how every person makes a difference, and some ways to reduce stress on the job. See Appendices 46, 47, 48 and 49.

The Vital Importance of Empowering and Rewarding Employees

CULTIVATION PHASE
Empowerment

"Management's job is to find out what it's doing that keeps people from doing a good job, and stop doing it."

Peter Drucker

It is imperative to reward employees based on their performance. As I have mentioned with regard to customers, employees should be treated as individuals. Across-the-board merit raises are archaic, because they communicate the idea that all employees are equal in their work, attitude, talents, etc. Not only is this not accurate, but it sends the message, "We really do **not** care about you or your work."

Thus, you should not reward employees who perform poorly. Focus on the positive things that your employees do, and hold them responsible and accountable for results. Make sure you reward people based on their actual results, not on how well they publicize and promote themselves. I know of a company that financially rewards the responsible employees when they obtain a new customer, and financially penalizes those responsible when a customer leaves. Now, that is an exciting place to work, because everyone is highly accountable!

Based on a 1997 study of 1500 employees, the most powerful motivation for employees is congratulations for a job well done from their bosses. Yet only 44% of bosses actually did this regularly.

Cash rewards and incentives lowered stress, absenteeism, and turnover, and raised morale, productivity, competitiveness, revenue and profits. Participants reported that when they recognized their employees:

- Employees were better motivated, in 90.5% of the companies,
- Employees' performance improved, in 84.4% of the companies,
- Employees received practical feedback, in 84.4% of the companies,
- Employees stated that communication made it easier for them to get their work done, in 80.3% of the companies, and
- Employees became more productive, in 77.7% of the companies.

The three worst motivators are:

1. "Cost of Living"-based pay adjustments
2. "Point Factor" job evaluation plans
3. "Midpoint Control"

The three best motivators are:

1. "Merit Pay" salary programs
2. "Annual 'bonus' plans" that do not fold into base salary
3. "Skill and Competence Pay" that avoids a singular focus on "jobs"

Peter Drucker, the management guru, has said, "Management's job is to find out what it is doing that keeps people from doing a good job, and stop doing it." Now that you know what the worst motivators are, stop using them! Concentrate your time and energy on using the most effective ways of supporting your employees in doing the best job they can do.

Empowerment is an overused word, and thus, I want to define what it means to me and how I will use it.

EMPOWERMENT

First, Give Employees the Tools They Need to Do Their Jobs...

Second, Remove Any Roadblocks...

Third, Get Out Of Their Way!

If Management wants empowered employees, it must hire for attitude and train for skills, continuously retrain employees, eliminate red tape, give employees the power to do their job, and then just get out of their way.

There are a few personal stories I want to relate as a way of illustrating the difference between an empowered and an unempowered employee, from the customer's perspective.

Several years ago, I was traveling from Los Angeles to Boston and was ticketed for a Northwest Flight. There were only fifteen of us, and we were asked if we would be willing to take an American Airlines flight that was scheduled to arrive in Boston about five minutes after our flight. We all agreed. I then tried to notify my friend Bob, who was going to pick me up at the airport, that I would be arriving on a different airline, one that arrives at a different terminal at Logan Airport in Boston. I called him at work, and had a written message left for him. Northwest said they would continue to call people we had not reached to ensure they would be waiting for us at Terminal B and not E. The flight arrived without a problem, but Bob was not there. I was unable to find personnel to help me page him. I then thought maybe he did not get the message and tried to page him at Northwest, but no one answered the telephone at the Northwest arrivals area. I waited 45 minutes and took a $40 taxi ride home. When I finally spoke to Bob, he said he never received the message at work. He said there was some confusion at Northwest; they knew we were on another flight, but not which one. So he went from parking lot to parking lot and checked every terminal; then he drove home. He spent $15 on parking lot fees. I was steamed.

The next morning, I called Northwest's 800 number, relayed the story the exactly as I just told it, and asked for a $55 refund. What do you think the representative said? Most people would expect to hear, "Forget it." I can still feel the impact of her words physically. She said, "No problem." What did that do to me? It disarmed me; it took the wind out of my sails. Why? Because I was expecting an argument, and remember, I am an attorney; I had a *prima facie* case—one that wins on the facts alone. I had the name of every person and every flight number. I was right! I was ready for a fight, but she did not oppose me.

The woman then said, "I cannot give you a refund, but I can give you a credit." I responded, "Fine." This is a very interesting reaction! Let us look at what happened in that interaction. If she had initially responded, "I cannot give you a refund. Would a credit be O.K.?" I would not have had as strong a positive reaction. The employee's gambit worked because she started by agreeing with me and making me right, not making me wrong. Clearly, employees need to be trained to skillfully disarm upset or angry customers. There are a few companies that do this superbly, and you cannot upset their employees; I know because I have tried. It would not surprise me to learn that this Northwest employee looked up how many miles I fly with Northwest and asked herself, "Do I give her a $55 credit or lose her?" She made the right decision, since I have told this story hundreds of times and they get free positive word-of-mouth advertising from it every time I tell it! For an example of the cost of complaints, and employee empowerment around complaints, see Appendix 50.

The next story is an experience I had on an American Airlines plane during a cross-country flight. I was seated in the exit row, and those seats do not recline. In order to see a monitor to view the movie I would have had to squash my face against the window since a tall man was blocking my view. Thus, when the flight attendant came through asking for five dollars for the headset, I commented I thought I should get it for free since it would be a challenge to see the movie from a non-reclining seat. She said, "Oh, I will go ask the Captain," and she walked away. At first, I thought that was well handled and then I sat upright, almost startled: I want the Captain to fly the airplane, not attend to a five-dollar item!

All sorts of negative thoughts were running through my head. Why could she not make a five-dollar decision? It seemed reasonable that she might need to ask the head flight attendant, and maybe, if absolutely necessary, the co-pilot, but **not** the Captain. When the flight attendant returned and said that all six people in the exit rows would receive the headsets free, I was not comforted.

So, if you do not have the authority to make a decision, do not advertise it to your customers. Say something like "Let me check on that."

The last story is around my experiences filing a claim for missing baggage with American Airlines. The woman working in this area seemed unhappy with her job, since she greeted me with a heavy sigh. She was annoyed that my baggage did not exactly match any of their pictures. The she asked me if I wanted my baggage delivered at 10:00 PM or 2:00 AM. I was not certain that I would be home by 10:00 PM, while 2:00 AM is in the middle of the night. She replied, "Those are the only options." I said, "There are others." She snapped, "Like what?" I said, "Well you could put it into a taxi," and she interrupted me, saying that was too expensive. I knew she did not know how many miles I fly, as did the Northwest Airlines representative. I then said, "Well, the Super Shuttle is $12.50, and they could bring it to the Newton Marriott, which is about a mile and a half from my home." She was getting flustered, and blurted out, "I do not know how to do that." I felt we were in a tug-of-war, and I was doing her job, trying to find an option that would work. I was getting increasingly frustrated. Finally, I said, "It would help if you had apologized that my baggage was lost at the beginning of our conversation." She responded, "Oh, I do that at the end." My jaw dropped.

This woman had been trained, but incorrectly. A person **must** empathize first and **then** move into solution mode. Since we know the answer to the person's question, most of us forget there is a human being who has been inconvenienced and who is upset. We rush to a resolution, and inadvertently run over the person's feelings. Remember that we need to first acknowledge the feelings, and then people will be the most open to and cooperative for the solution mode.

If the baggage claim woman had said, "I am sorry your baggage did not arrive with you. Let's see what we can do to get it back in your hands ASAP," or, "I can understand why you are upset. I would be, too, if my baggage did not arrive with me," I would have been more understanding and helpful. That would not be an admission of wrongdoing, but an acknowledgement that a human being is not happy. Starting with empathy translates to easier resolutions when you want to delight customers.

Some key points on handling angry customers: First, do not talk faster or louder than they are talking. That will just exacerbate the situation. Always, speak more softly and more slowly. Mentally apply the word Grandma to everything you say to an angry customer. If you would not say it to your grandmother, then do not say it to a customer. Know that the customer is always right; s/he may not be accurate, but s/he is always right. If you had lived life in that person's shoes, you would have the same response. Sometimes an angry customer just wants to be listened to. So if you have one that is just speaking a mile a minute, actively listen to him/her. Do not leave long empty spaces, but instead fill them with encouraging words like "I get it," "Yes," "Uh, huh," "OK." This will let the customer know you are listening. At some point the person needs to take a breath and will stop. You can respond, "Thank you for telling me all of that. I want to tell you what I heard, to make sure I got everything correct, so we can straighten this out ASAP. OK?" Then active listen[2] back to the customer what s/he said. That is enough for some people. They just want someone to care enough to listen to them and not interrupt them.

Make sure that, along the path to your goals, you take the time to celebrate the small wins along the way. The best companies wisely look for reasons, even silly reasons, to celebrate something. Make achieving goals fun!

Some have adopted a victory bell that is rung for each new sale. Some ring it once for each $1,000 of a sale. Be creative and aim to get people to laugh. Laughter is a great stress-reducer, and can work wonders during stressful times.

---

2 Active listening is a listening technique where you repeat back to the speaker what you heard him/her say. It allows the speaker to know s/he was heard, and is a terrific way to calm an upset customer. It also allows the listener to be sure s/he has all the pertinent details.

Wow!ing Customers for Life

THE CUSTOMER RETENTION GRID

Your "highly satisfied" customers are **six** times more likely to repurchase the same product, cross-buy and refer.

Outcome			
Value Added	At Risk	★ Loyal	Advocate! ★
Expectations Met	Searching	At Risk	★ Loyal
Expectations Not Met	Gone	Searching	At Risk
	Dissatisfied	Satisfied	Dazzled

Process

This Customer Retention grid illustrates the two components of each interaction: a process and outcome. The grid illustrates the conditions that are needed to satisfy customers and make them loyal—but, of course, you will set your sights higher than mere satisfaction and loyalty! How can you dazzle and delight your customers, and turn them into "Advocates"? Customers need two conditions met to become Advocates: first, they must be dazzled by the process, and second, they must experience an outcome where their expectations are far exceeded to the point where they receive added value. Most companies do not elicit a customer's expectations, and thus do not know how they are doing in their attempts to meet those expectations. This is critical information that takes only moments to obtain. Ask your customers what they expect as the outcome of an interaction, and in what time period.

We need to gather feedback from our customers, our employees and our vendors and to create a much more interactive work environment, so we can take advantage of all opportunities to excel. Listen closely, very closely to your market. There are two primary methods of gathering feedback: qualitative and quantitative. The purpose of the former is to gather as many new ideas as possible, while the purpose of the latter is to test those ideas to uncover which ones are statistically valid and reliable. Many companies only conduct one type of data gathering. This is much less than ideal. In fact, it leads to bias and distorted data. It is best to have the qualitative drive the quantitative, since the qualitative encompasses most perspectives and is guided by the customers' input.

Focus groups are the most common tool for the qualitative stage, but they are overused and can be the most ineffective tool. They suffer from group-think: one person mentions an idea or perspective, and most of the others in the group follow suit rather than expressing their own individual ideas. On the other hand, focus groups are the best method to create a totally new product or service. They are superb in that area!

If you want to improve upon an existing product or service, conduct retention analysis to understand why customers behave as they do. Interview a variety of people, including frontline employees, to produce powerful, targeted information for a survey. The best methods of obtaining useful information are in-person interviews and telephone interviews.

In an interview situation, the interviewer needs to probe four to five levels beneath the interviewee's initial response to reach the root cause of a customer's behavior. The root cause will usually be something that the frontline person needs to either do more of or do less of. The interviewing technique takes much skill and experience, since it is vital that the interviewee does not experience the interviewer as pushy or overbearing. Thus the interviewer needs to know when and how much to probe, and especially, what non-verbal signals indicate that the interviewer should stop and/or circle back later. Skillfully utilizing a variety of qualitative methods to develop the quantitative survey ensures a higher response rate, and ensures results that are specific and implementable.

In the qualitative stage, I strongly recommend that companies work with market researchers who interview the frontline employees, any middle service people and several customers **before** drafting a telephone survey or written survey. This process produces surveys with very high response rates, since the responses are in the customers' own words.

If I had not interviewed the "A" guests of the Hyatt Regency in Cambridge, I would not have ever known about C.J. and Andrew. Some guests would have probably written about C.J. and Andrew in their responses to a paper survey, but the full impact of these two men would not have been as obvious or clear.

What types of information would be valuable for you to gather from Current Customers, Former Customers and Employees? Come up with a list of at least ten different questions whose answers would give you an advantage over your competitors who have not asked these questions.

Complaints Are the Tip of the Iceberg

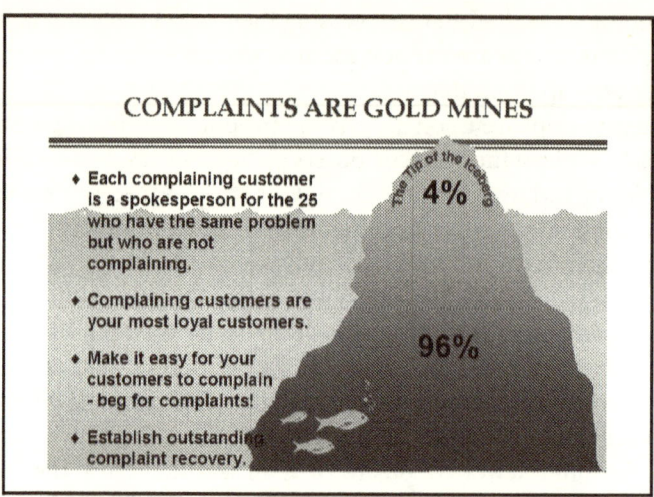

Many studies have revealed the same startling statistics: four percent of customers complain, while the rest walk away quietly. In many cases, you do not even know that they have left. Only 4% complain! Thus your complaining customers are your **most** loyal customers. They are giving you the gift of their precious time, and each one freely offers a gold mine of feedback to help your company to excel! Underneath the complaint, each complaining customer is saying, "Please help me to stay. I want to stay." It may not be said gracefully or kindly, but remember that the customer did take the time to call. That speaks volumes about the value the customer places on his or her relationship with your company.

As businesspeople, we all want to hear from customers if they are not happy. Yet most customers will not complain. Why? Several classic reasons account for this:

1. The customer thinks it will not make a difference.
2. The customer does not like confrontation.
3. The customer does not know who to complain to.
4. The customer believes no one really cares.

In response, companies must counter these perceptions with a strong message that they really **do** care. A company must make it clear that it will respond to customer concerns, that giving feedback and making complaints is easy and painless, and that the company really wants customer feedback. So make it easy for customers to complain. The proliferation of 800 numbers illustrates the awareness of this reality that most companies now have. You cannot afford to make it difficult for customers to complain, because it will give customers another reason to just quietly walk away.

Of course, there is a difference between complaining customers and chronic complainers; I am speaking about the former. If you have had an "A" customer that you have not heard from in a while, call that customer and proactively ask how things are going. No one is happy for that long! Be daring, be willing to hear about and respond to what is not working, and show that you care!

GE, GM, Polaroid and AMEX have turned their complaint centers into profit centers. Their ROI for these centers has ranged from 15% to 401%. If these companies, which usually remain remote from their end-users, are now reaching out and proactively contacting those customers, you should, too. Learn from those companies that have extensively used market research to find the most effective ways to increase customer retention. Follow their lead.

GE calls 14,000 customers a week to ask how they like the new appliance they just purchased. Wow! As a consumer, I have always thought that the sale was between the retailer and me. I never thought GE would call me! A number of years ago, I mentioned this during a speaking engagement, and a man raised his hand and said, "I received one of those calls last week." I asked him how he currently felt toward GE. He said, "They care, while the rest of the manufacturers do not. I will always go to GE first." With that single telephone call, GE not only created a customer for life, but also—perhaps, more importantly—raised the bar for all of its competitors. It has become the benchmark for those customers who received a call.

That is what I want my clients to do: do the tango when everyone else is doing the twist. Stand out in a positive way from the crowd.

The good news about complaining customers is that a fair resolution of a complaint will easily Wow! them. For example, imagine that you dropped off five shirts at the dry cleaners, and the next day you picked them up and found that while four were perfect, the fifth was missing a button. When you pointed it out, the clerk said, "No problem, we will fix it, and it will be ready tomorrow." You returned the next day and the shirt was fine. Is your level of loyalty higher or lower because of this interaction? It is higher. But why? The company only did what it was initially expected to do!

The fact is that when we complain, we are usually treated so poorly that when someone treats us decently, we are thrilled. Thus, if a customer complains and you do only what was initially expected, it is equivalent of a "5" on the satisfaction scale—and doing what was initially expected should be a very easy thing to accomplish. Therefore, I tell my clients to beg for complaints. These customers are taking their precious time to offer you free market research. Send them Thank-you notes for complaining. That will Wow! them!

Nordstrom's is known for hiring high-quality salespeople and empowering them to use their best judgement. The company has no rulebook. A man returned a tire to Nordstrom's. When the salesperson asked for a receipt, he said he did not have it. The salesperson ask what he had paid for the tire and the man said $75. She gave him a $75 refund. Sounds OK, but there is a catch. Nordstrom's does not even sell tires! So, why did the salesperson give the man a refund? Most likely, she did not want to embarrass him and possibly lose him as a customer. At some point in the future, he may realize that he did not purchase the tire at Nordstrom's, and he will probably be forever grateful that the salesperson treated him with dignity and respect.

Once you have customers complaining, you need to have excellent complaint recovery in place. A well-known example of outstanding complaint recovery took place with a group of people on a chartered airplane heading from La Guardia Airport in New York to Club Med at Cancun, Mexico for February school vacation. Everything imaginable went wrong on this flight. The pilot tried to take off twice, but he slammed on the brakes both times before they took off. Each time, he announced they would try again in a couple hours once the brakes cooled.

Then there was a thunderstorm. An airplane is much safer on the runway than back at the gate in a thunderstorm, so they waited out the storm. The pilot needed to limit the amount of heat on the airplane since that would use fuel and he did not want to have to go back and refuel. Eight hours passed and the airplane was cold, there was no more food or drinks, and the bathrooms had an unpleasant odor. Two attorneys aboard were taking names for a class action suit. The flight was not even off the ground and things were looking grim.

The airplane finally took off, and it was a bumpy ride for much of the trip because of the weather. The landing was rough and many oxygen masks fell out. The passengers had finally arrived, but they were not a happy bunch. Fortunately for Club Med, one of its best General Managers was working at this Club. He had received word of the problems with the flight. He could have said to himself, "This is not my problem; it is a chartered flight." However, he was wise enough to know that if he did not act, these people would be talking about their negative experiences with the other guests at his hotel for the next week, which would have a significant negative impact on all of the guests.

He stayed with the basics. He figured the passengers needed food, drinks and a clean bathroom. He had each person escorted off the plane, given food and drinks on the runway, and ushered to the bathroom and then through customs. Once they arrived at the Resort, he arranged for a Mariachi band, and free food and drinks until dawn. He had struck a bargain with the other guests: if they would stay up until 2 AM to be there when the new guests arrived, he would give them free drinks all night. They said, "Sure," and everyone partied until dawn, and said they had the best time since college.

What do you think these new guests talked about with their friends and family when they returned home? The party, of course! They probably mentioned having a really hard time getting to the resort, but the complaint recovery was outstanding and thus the original complaint slipped into the background of each person's mind.

Complaint resolution is an art, and it must be done sensitively and skillfully in order to be effective. For some examples of phrases that never should be spoken to customers, see Appendix 51; for telephone tips and common-sense customer recovery strategies, see Appendices 52 and 53.

THE VALUE OF QUICK RESOLUTION

Industry	Needs only 1 Contact	Needs 2 or More Contacts
Auto Repairs/Service	50%	18%
Computers	68%	28%
Financial Services	56%	22%
Hotel	46%	13%
Industrial Sales	86%	42%
Packaged Goods	77%	40%
Retail Banking	66%	35%

Since nowadays, speed is not only valued but also required, the first person a customer speaks with at a company needs to be empowered to resolve the problem. This chart illustrates that if the first person resolves the problem, regardless of the industry, a higher percentage of customers will rate their experience a "5" on a one-to-five-point scale. When the customer is transferred to a second person or needs to wait 24 hours or more for resolution, the number of people rating their satisfaction a "5" declines significantly, regardless of the industry. For an example of the cost of unresolved complaints, see Appendix 54.

Summary of Cultivation Phase

- Wow! employees to establish a solid foundation for Wow!ed customers.
- Create only customer advocates.
- Conduct qualitative and quantitative research to keep abreast of your customers' changing expectations and needs.
- Uncover those "Moments of Truth" that keep your company from being highly profitable.
- Make it easy for customers to complain, and reward those that do.
- Record, categorize and uncover the root causes of the complaints. Then eliminate those root causes.
- Become outstanding at complaint recovery.

Winning Customers Back— Reactivation Stage

There are some basic steps in this Phase. A company must do the following:

1. Decide whom it wants to win back.
2. Ask customers what happened that led to their decision to leave.
3. Find out how to win them back.
4. Develop a written plan to win them back.
5. Then win them back!

The best time period to win customers back is within two to three years of their leaving your company. Why? Because the customers are going through the Assimilation Phase with a new company and are most vulnerable to leaving. Stay in contact with them at least through this Assimilation Phase.

When a profitable customer leaves, I recommend you call him/her immediately and say, "I am sorry that you have decided to leave, and respect your decision. I want you to know that I care about you and your business. Since we have been working together for _____ years, I know your business well. Please call me with any questions, or to bounce an idea off me. Consider me your advisor. I want to make sure you have the proper coverage. Best of luck, and I hope this new situation will work better for you." The former customer will be stunned, mostly because you did not attempt to get his business back. You positioned yourself as a trusted advisor, and that is the beast way to regain a former customer. Then call two more times, about three months apart, and say you are checking in to make sure that the customer is happy. Call again if you have some information that indicates that the customer is not happy. Ask if you may review the coverage the customer has, and see if it make sense to work together again. Continue this method of regular contact until there is an opening, and then get the customer back!

Winbacks—Smart, Profitable Strategies

One of the key reasons it is financially prudent to try to win back "A" customers who have defected is that there are only a limited number of "A" customers in any given location. Winback programs offer a competitive edge: the average business has a 20% to 40% probability of successfully selling to lost customers, compared to a 5% to 20% probability of making a sale to prospective customers.

Winback programs offer support for your company's acquisition and retention efforts. However, without winback-related data, your company may be spending money chasing and retaining the wrong types of customers.

So why is this approach so effective?

1. Customers who have defected are already familiar with your company's products and services.
2. You already have information about these customers' preferences.
3. You have the ability to personally address these customers in your winback effort (unlike your colleagues in marketing, who must contact virtual strangers as new prospects for your business).

Winback strategies work! For an article that addresses how to create a winback strategy, see Appendix 55.

Reasons Customers Leave–They are Not What You Think!

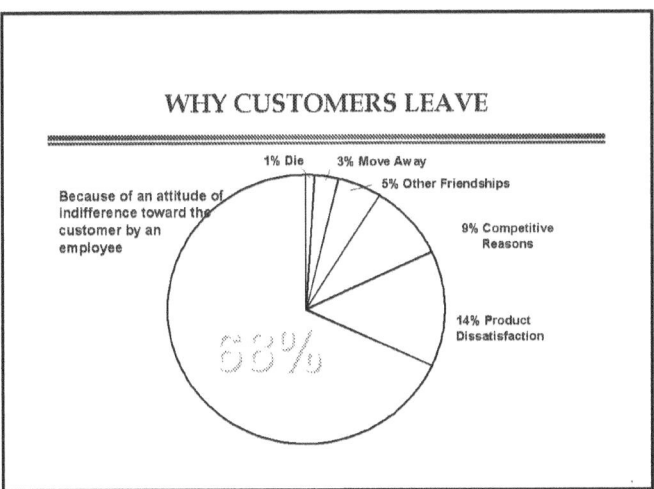

WHY CUSTOMERS LEAVE

1% Die   3% Move Away

5% Other Friendships

Because of an attitude of indifference toward the customer by an employee

9% Competitive Reasons

14% Product Dissatisfaction

68%

The number one reason customers leave any business is because someone at the company did not show that he or she cared. A human being showed indifference toward the customer. Sadly, indifference is rampant in our society.

More than two-thirds of customers walk out the door for this reason! Three sources arrived at the same figure, plus or minus one percent, for percentage of customers who leave due to the perception that people at a company are indifferent to customers: *Fortune* magazine, *U.S. News & World Report* and the American Bar Association. Therefore, it is crucial for you to know exactly what to do so your "A" customers will know that you care about them. Do not leave this to luck, guessing or happenstance; it is too risky. Ask customers what would make them know they are cared about, and make this one of the initial questions that is consistently asked of a new customer. Be sure this information is added to each customer's list of preferences, so you are customizing your interactions to ensure every customer feels cared about!

Some upsets are avoidable; see Appendix 56 for guidelines.

The general myth is that price is the reason customers leave. When surveyed, 42% of customers claim to be leaving because of price. 38% leave for non-controllable reasons (for example, a company goes out of business or merges with another company) and the remaining 20% leave for controllable reasons (for example, "My telephone calls were not returned," or "When I complained, I felt I was a bother"). However, when we dug down deeper in our interviews with former customers, a different picture emerged. The root causes underneath their initial responses were categorized as follows: price was a major factor for only 23%, and this was one of four to five reasons needed for a customer to leave; 29% had left for non-controllable reasons, while 48% had left for controllable reasons.

Why do many people say "price" when asked why they left? Because price is an easy way to say good-bye. There is no easy response that you can offer to have them return. If they said, "The last three times I called and left a message, it took three days to get a response," you could reply, "We just hired a new receptionist," and they might feel hooked and be in an uncomfortable position. But price is indisputable.

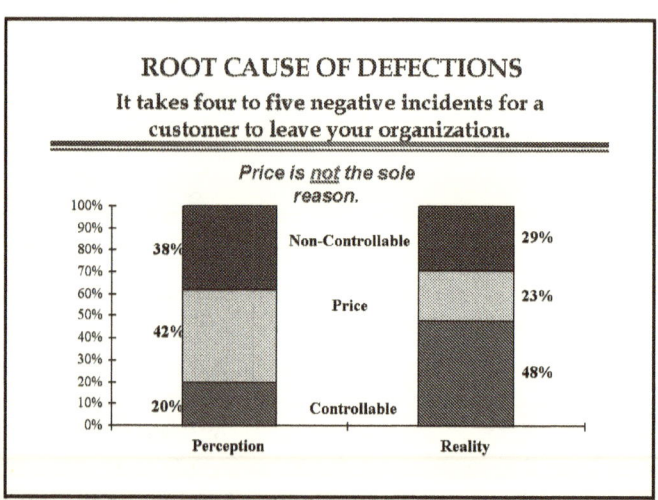

It takes four to five negative experiences for a customer to leave any company. People are loyal by nature and do not want to change—we would rather everything just work out smoothly with our current vendors. This is true of all of your current customers. However, companies have "coffee stains" (refer back to "The Powerful Upside Potential of Customer Retention") that literally chase customers away.

Although people may insist that a customer left because of price, that is at best only part of the story. I have interviewed thousand of former customers, and I would say maybe 5% to 7% left solely for price, and the price differential was more than 10% to 15%. We are generally willing to pay 10% to 15% more for high-quality products and services. If a customer leaves your company for less, s/he is sending you the message, "I do not believe I am receiving high-quality products and services." If your company provides high-quality products and services, not only does your company receive this extra premium, but it will also grow twice as fast as those that do not, and it will gain about 6% of market share rather than losing about 2% per year.

Why do companies fail to hear the voice of their customers? There are some common pitfalls. See Appendix 57.

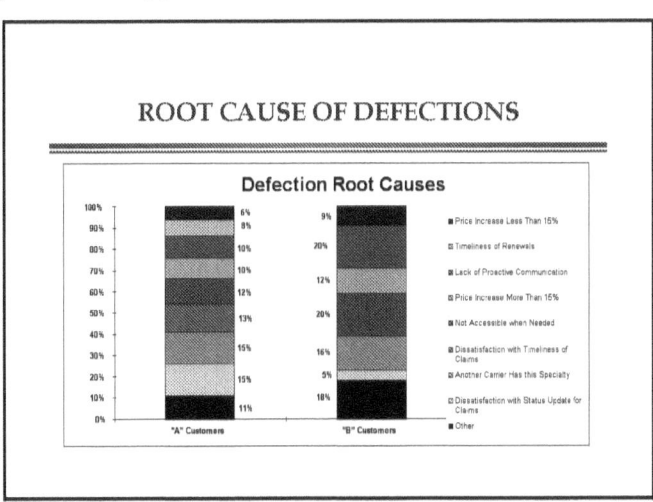

This is an example of how market research can benefit your company. The "A" customers in this company want to receive status reports on claims that exceed $10,000. Thus, when an employee interacts with an "A" customer, he knows that he must either supply regular status updates, or risk significantly increasing the likelihood that the customer will leave. On the other hand, a "B" customer in this company is much more likely to leave if he does not receive ample proactive contact. Same company, but two different types of customers, and two different reasons for leaving. With this type of data, your employees are empowered to tailor their interactions to Wow! your customers.

Partial Defectors and the Early Defection Warning System

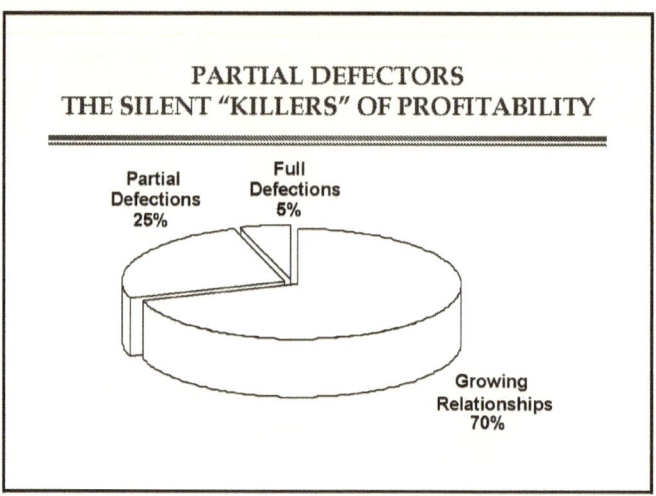

**PARTIAL DEFECTORS
THE SILENT "KILLERS" OF PROFITABILITY**

Partial Defections 25%

Full Defections 5%

Growing Relationships 70%

Many companies only track customers and defectors. When working with a bank, I noticed they had a third category: diminishers. A customer who diminishes his or her balances by a certain percentage, or closes a certain number of accounts, fits into this category. These customers have, in effect, partially left the company. Partial defection is a critical area that most businesses are not aware of. Approximately 25% of your customers partially left your company this year, and unless you can identify them, it is likely that within the next few years, they will become former customers. Customers may have diminished their business for a reason that is within your company's control. The companies that are aware of diminishers are able to intervene, and to rectify a situation that would otherwise probably go unnoticed, ultimately driving away customers. If factors outside of your control are causing partial defections, that is also good to know, since the same situation may occur with other customers. In these cases, factors that **are** in your control—the interactions customers have with your company—need to be truly superb.

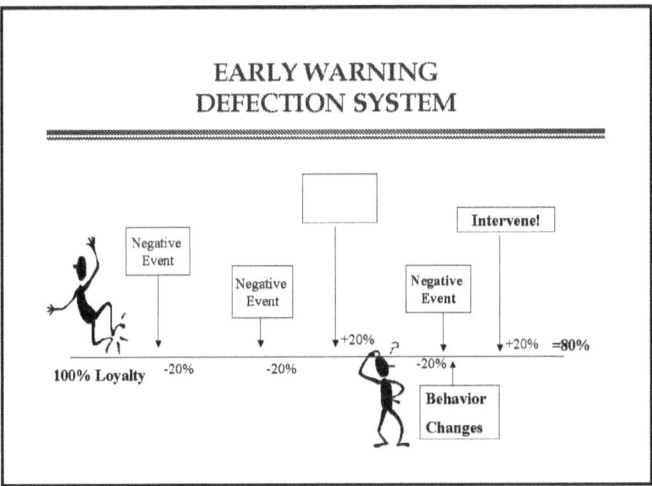

How would you like to be able to predict when a customer is about to leave, even before the customer himself is absolutely certain he is about to leave? Does this sound like a fantasy? This is possible with today's technology. It is called an Early Defection Warning System (also known as a Defection Prevention Plan). Customers are profiled and, based on their behaviors, a company can predict with approximately 85% certainty when a customer will defect. This provides the company with time to intervene and keep its "A" customers. That is a godsend, since most companies are able to retain over 90% of these customers if the companies are warned and have time to intervene. However, if companies fail to act, almost all of these customers will leave, taking their lifetime value (revenue) with them.

Consider this sample profile of a customer who is at risk of defection:

- The customer has been with the company for less than 18 months
- The customer has spent less than $5,000
- The customer's business has a profit margin of less than 5%
- The customer has switched other vendors more than once in the past three years

To understand how an Early Defection Warning System works, see Appendices 58, 59 and 60.

The next step is to identify the reasons customers leave, and divide those reasons into two categories: controllable and uncontrollable. No company will have 100% retention forever, since things are changing all the time: businesses move out of state, go out of business, or merge, while individuals within a company may move out of state, decide they need a change, retire, or die. It is important to define the controllable reasons that customers leave, and focus a company's efforts on these.

The final step is identifying pre-defection warning signs. These are the signs that frontline people must look for that indicate that a customer is in danger of defection, because he is behaving like other customers who have left the company. Being aware of these signs will give you the opportunity to intervene and keep the customer who is considering defection.

When a customer purchases a product, s/he is deemed to be 100% loyal. For each negative event, his/her loyalty declines by 20%, while for each positive event, it increases by 20%. If the customer's loyalty drops to approximately 50%, his/her behavior will change, and that can be detected, allowing a company to intervene to retain that customer.

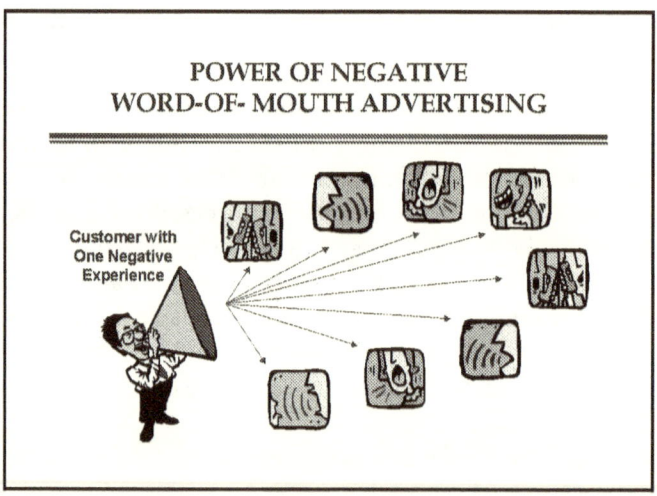

Negative word-of-mouth advertising about "small" negative experiences is awesomely powerful. Most people will tell an average of eight to ten people about every negative event they experience. One out of ten people will tell twenty others. That averages to eleven people who are told about every negative event. When resultant changes in loyalty are factored in, a company loses an average of 2.4 customers for every negative event.

On the other hand, for every positive event we experience, we will tell three or four others. Calculating on the basis of four people hearing about every positive event, a company gains an average of 1.2 customers for each positive event. We lose twice as many customers for each negative event as we gain for each positive event. Think about the impact that your behavior can have in your marketplace the next time you lose your patience, or treat a customer in a less-than-courteous manner.

> *"The real voyage of discovery consists not in seeking new landscapes, but in having new eyes."*
>
> -Marcel Proust

The real voyage is not in seeking new landscapes but having new eyes. We must learn to see what we never saw before and notice the things we usually miss (like the two "the"s in the exercise on page 32 and the many letter "F"s in the exercise on page 33). We need to find solutions that are "outside the box." Welcome to the world of business in this new millennium!

Part II

Appendix 1: Reality Check for Customer and Employee Retention

Purpose: Assessment of your current Customer Retention practices will assist in identifying both your business' strengths and its opportunities for improvement.

On a scale of "1" to "5," where "1" is <u>poor</u> and "5" is <u>excellent</u>, how would you rate your company on the following?

Business Realities/Paradigms	Poor			Excellent	
Viewing readiness to change as key component of your success?	1	2	3	4	5
Benchmarking your company against companies outside of your industry	1	2	3	4	5
Meeting customers' requests for customization	1	2	3	4	5
Staying current with market trends and development	1	2	3	4	5
Realigning business to focus on building relationships rather than selling products	1	2	3	4	5
Hiring employees who easily embrace change	1	2	3	4	5
Focusing on delivering speed, accuracy and expertise	1	2	3	4	5
Establishing relationships with your customers that only God can break	1	2	3	4	5
Attending trade meetings of other industries to learn about their best practices	1	2	3	4	5
Establishing formal mechanisms to gather customer and employee feedback on how you can improve	1	2	3	4	5
Truly valuing and implementing customer and employee feedback	1	2	3	4	5
Regularly involving customers in your improvement process	1	2	3	4	5
Adding at least one non-traditional value-added service or product to meet your customers' needs every year	1	2	3	4	5

Segmentation	Poor			Excellent	
Identifying your business' distinct markets	1	2	3	4	5
Segmenting your markets into "A," "B" and "C" customers	1	2	3	4	5
Focusing 50% or more of your time on "A" customers	1	2	3	4	5
Identifying your top ten "A" customers	1	2	3	4	5

Customer Retention Business Analysis	Poor			Excellent	
Knowing the top five reasons your "A" customers do business with your company	1	2	3	4	5
Having a Customer Retention strategy that utilizes your unique competitive advantages	1	2	3	4	5
Clearly identifying the reasons your "A" customers came, have stayed with and would leave your business	1	2	3	4	5
Having a Customer Relationship Management plan to ensure that your "A" customers are "Wow!"ed	1	2	3	4	5
Having a Customer Relationship Management plan for upgrading "B"s to "A"s and "C"s to "B"s	1	2	3	4	5
Having Producers working only with "A" and "B" accounts, and internal staff working with "C" accounts	1	2	3	4	5
Consistently conducting market research to know your customers' expectations	1	2	3	4	5
Keeping current with technology needs	1	2	3	4	5
Reducing the rework	1	2	3	4	5
Identifying your company's added value	1	2	3	4	5

Acquisition Phase	Poor			Excellent	
Identifying your top ten prospects	1	2	3	4	5
Having standardized sales proposals	1	2	3	4	5
Knowing the lifetime value of your "A" customers	1	2	3	4	5
Having marketing and selling materials that include the reasons customers have said they decided to do business with you	1	2	3	4	5
Having established sales and service performance standards	1	2	3	4	5
Establishing a proactive process for "A" and "B" prospects	1	2	3	4	5
Super-qualifying your prospects to identify "A" and "B" clients before going out on the sales call	1	2	3	4	5
Having a formal sales process	1	2	3	4	5
Having a formally-named Sales Manager	1	2	3	4	5
Acquiring 85% to 90% of new business from referrals	1	2	3	4	5
Having a compensation structure that rewards more for "A" and "B" referrals than for "C" referrals	1	2	3	4	5
Rehearsing sales presentations for "A" and "B" customers	1	2	3	4	5
Debriefing after sales presentations to "A" and "B" customers	1	2	3	4	5

Assimilation Phase	Poor			Excellent	
Offering your "A" customers an orientation ("Welcome Aboard!") package	1	2	3	4	5
Thoroughly explaining who will support the customer when service begins	1	2	3	4	5
Proactively contacting customers shortly after a service problem arises	1	2	3	4	5
Weekly, sending a minimum of ten handwritten thank-you notes to "A" customers	1	2	3	4	5
Designing your web page to retain customers	1	2	3	4	5

Cultivation Phase	Poor				Excellent
Having employees proactively cultivate relationships with customers	1	2	3	4	5
Having a formal system in place to contact "A" and "B" customers on a regular basis	1	2	3	4	5
Having a process so that customers always know who you are, what you do, and what you offer them	1	2	3	4	5
Rewarding employees for cross-selling	1	2	3	4	5
Hiring for attitude and training for skills	1	2	3	4	5
Eliminating roadblocks to employees' effectiveness	1	2	3	4	5
Seeking and respecting employee input and ideas	1	2	3	4	5
Developing options for employees to address the balance of life issues	1	2	3	4	5
Offering employee performance reviews at least quarterly	1	2	3	4	5
Developing fun and outrageous ways to celebrate the "wins" along the way	1	2	3	4	5
Investing in employee training	1	2	3	4	5
Focusing on "Wow!"ing and delighting employees	1	2	3	4	5
Reselling your business' added-value with each customer contact	1	2	3	4	5
Having every person involved in direct customer contact actively seeking to learn more about the customers' needs	1	2	3	4	5
Regularly logging and updating "A" customer's service preferences and then using them to cement these relationships	1	2	3	4	5
Having every employee make each Customer Retention contact a positive experience for the customer	1	2	3	4	5
Regularly debriefing "A" customers after significant service events to uncover ways to improve the processes	1	2	3	4	5
Having a plan to create "raving-fan customers" who will sell your business for you	1	2	3	4	5
Consistently asking for referrals to the extent that it is a reflexive behavior	1	2	3	4	5
"Begging" your customers for complaints	1	2	3	4	5
Making it easy for customers to complain	1	2	3	4	5
Tracking and categorizing complaints and eliminating the root causes	1	2	3	4	5
Having a superior complaint recovery process	1	2	3	4	5

Reactivation Phase	Poor				Excellent
Knowing when a customer is about to *stop doing* business with you	1	2	3	4	5
Staying in contact with former "A" customers	1	2	3	4	5
Having a system in place to find out why "A" customers left	1	2	3	4	5
Developing a Defection Prevention Plan	1	2	3	4	5
Identifying partial defectors, and developing and implementing an intervention plan	1	2	3	4	5
Knowing how many "A" customers your business lost last year and the revenue they represented	1	2	3	4	5
Using Client Councils to win back customers	1	2	3	4	5

What are the strengths and opportunities for improvement for your company in its Customer Retention practices?

<u>Strengths</u>	<u>Opportunities for Improvement</u>
_____	_____
_____	_____
_____	_____
_____	_____
_____	_____
_____	_____

Scoring:

(Number of "1"s) _____ x 1 = _____

(Number of "2"s) _____ x 2 = _____

(Number of "3"s) _____ x 3 = _____

(Number of "4"s) _____ x 4 = _____

(Number of "5"s) _____ x 5 = _____

Total Score   = _____

Evaluation:

390	=	<u>Perfect</u> Score!!	= 25%+ Annual Profit Growth
330	=	"Wow!"	= 20%–24% Annual Profit Growth
295	=	Very Good	= 15%–19% Annual Profit Growth
265	=	Good	= 10%–14% Annual Profit Growth
235	=	Average	= 5%–9% Annual Profit Growth

Appendix 2: Customer Service that "Wow!"s—Max's Laws

1. This restaurant is run for the enjoyment and pleasure of our customers, not the convenience of the staff or the owners.
2. You get a free round of drinks if anyone on our staff comes up and says "Is everything all right?" When we ask questions, they'll be good ones.
3. You must get your mustard and ketchup before your burger, sandwich or fries.
4. We hate soggy fries. If yours aren't crisp, the way you like them, send them back. The kitchen will get the message.
5. Corned beef and pastrami are good because they contain some fat; however, with today's diet-consciousness, our corned beef and pastrami are now extra lean. So ask for a little fat for that traditional taste. If you want something with no fat, how about our turkey or turkey pastrami?
6. The turkey is always fresh. Period.
7. Our iced tea is table-brewed. Just pour it over a big glass of ice.
8. You'll love our breads and pastries. They are made fresh daily in Max's Bakery and Kitchen.
9. Warning: We bake our own sourdough crusty as can be. If you like soft bread, eat the middle.
10. Our ice cream sauces are a point of pride. They're made in New York by a certified chocoholic who refuses therapy. They are simply the best in the country. And we don't boast idly.
11. We bring ice cream sauces from New York City. Eat here. Save the airfare.
12. This is a bad place for a diet and a good place for a diet.
13. Our desserts are excessive because nothing succeeds like excess. We encourage sharing if you're not super-hungry.
14. Substitutions are okay by us. Don't be bashful; you've got a mouth—use it.
15. We use cholesterol-free oil for frying and sautéing; anything can be grilled fat-free.
16. If you are a single diner and are greeted with the expression, "Just one?" dinner is on us.

17. We agree that the customer is always right. If there is a problem with your food or service, call for the manager—we'll fix it in a flash. But if you finish your plate, it couldn't have been all that bad, now, could it!?
18. If, upon presentation of your check, your server asks, "Do you want change?" you can forget about leaving a tip.

Who is Max? Max is my father: If he were alive today, he'd probably love our corned beef, and maybe he'd be proud of his boy for running restaurants the best he knows how.

Appendix 3: Top Ten "A" Customers

	Name	Company	Date Last Contacted	Next Call Date
1				
2				
3				
4				
5				
6				
7				
8				
9				
10				

Appendix 4: Now, That's a "Wow!"

Recently I had a small scratch and a dent on my car. Nothing serious. So, I went to a local body shop seeking an estimate, and heard, "Sorry, we're too busy to give you an estimate today. You need an appointment." Needless to say, I went looking for another body shop. As fate would have it, I saw Troppoli Collision Repair on a highway traveling home one afternoon (I remembered a catchy jingle of theirs on the radio.)

I pulled in. There, I was greeted by the owner:

"Coffee? That's not a bad dent at all, but the paint is a hard color to match—but I can do it. I'll have your estimate in five minutes for you. We're a direct repair shop for your carrier, ITT Hartford. If you like, I can file an estimate and get approval for you by tomorrow morning. Care to make an appointment for Monday to make the repair?"

Needless to say I made an appointment. The shop had my car for the four-day period they had told me they would need it, then delivered the car on time and in apparently perfect condition! I thanked the owner, Rich, and got in my car to drive away.

Oh no, trouble! My car was pulling to the left. I returned to the shop and spoke to Rich, who immediately test-drove my car and had it up on a rack in three minutes. He examined it and concluded that an error had been made. In an effort to evenly distribute the paint on my side panel, his body mechanic had jacked the car up from the rear wheel rather than from the center area. "Mr. Cerone, I am extremely embarrassed and sorry. No excuses. This is clearly my fault and I will repair it. I have already ordered a rental—at no cost to you—and will repair your car with original dealer parts in one day."

Guess what? Rich repaired it and delivered it back to me as good as new. Only one additional small problem: my wheel alignment was now off due to a new part. I didn't notice until I drove my car on the highway to Pennsylvania several days later. I took my car to the Acura dealer and asked them to perform an alignment. Then I sent Rich Troppoli the bill and suggested he consider reimbursing me.

One day later a letter arrived: "Mr. Cerone, I value your business and I am sorry for the inconvenience we caused you. Enclosed is a check for your wheel alignment. In twenty-five years in business this is the first time Troppoli has ever made a mistake of this nature. The body mechanic involved has been spoken with and he has agreed to be extremely careful to avoid repeating this mistake. Please consider using my services again, and thank you for your understanding."

Rich Troppoli made me say "Wow!" Rich Troppoli has a customer for life.

Regards,
Chuck Cerone

Appendix 5: How to Create a Compelling Story

The essence of a compelling buying experience is "surprising and delighting" your customers, asserts Tim Sanders, chief solutions officer at Yahoo. Here are six ways a company can provide a compelling buying experience every time it touches the customer or market:

1. **A perspective that encourages seeing product or service as an experience**
   What does it take to heighten or make that experience more compelling? It may require better service, more informed or engaging salespeople, etc.

2. **Company identity**
   This includes logos, fonts, or any vehicle that affects the way customers see your brand, or hear about it.

3. **People**
   Everyone who works at your company touches the market at some point and has some kind of exchange with the customer. It could be a customer service representative, salesperson, or a business development person. Do employees give the impression that working with customers is a compelling experience or that it is drudgery?

4. **Mass media**
   This is the medium used to create the experience. It include advertising (print, TV, or radio) and public relations.

5. **New media**
   You can create a strong Web presence by offering Web-casting, online events, or email campaigns, for example.

6. **Co-branding**
   Who or what you put your brand next to is critical because it creates an experience customers remember.

Source: *Executive Report on Customer Retention*, February 15, 2002

Appendix 6: Customer Loyalty Builds Profits[3]

- Just "satisfying" customers is not enough; annually 15% to 40% of "satisfied" customers defect from the institutions they have been using.

- The objective for marketers is "totally satisfied" customers. They are six times as likely to re-purchase from you over a one-to five-year period.

- A 5% reduction in customer defections annually can increase profits 30% to 85%! Said another way, a 20% increase in retention is the equivalent of a 10% reduction in operating expenses.

- Marketing to, and obtaining, new customers is expensive—five to seven times more expensive than retaining current clients. Customer loyalty is measured two-dimensionally:
    - ® by intentions, attitudes, and perceptions
    - ® by actions

- Totally satisfied customers bring in profits five ways:
    - ® base sale
    - ® cross-selling/upselling
    - ® price premiums
    - ® referrals
    - ® lower operating costs.

- SHC "Loyalty Architecture" focuses on customers and employees. The employee side features hiring and retaining the right people, aligning your team around a shared purpose, equipping employees to confidently per-

---

3 Excerpt taken from the Fall 1998 issue of *BMA/NE The Marketplace*. Presenter: Susan Hodgkinson

form their jobs, involving them in improvement efforts, recognizing and rewarding them. The customer side includes listening to customers and the market, defining your value propositions, conducting targeted and needs-based selling, following up sales with rigorous service and after-marketing, superior problem resolution, accurate measurement processes followed up by appropriate actions.

Appendix 7: Limitations of Customer Satisfaction Survey Data

When faced with increasing competition and market maturation, suppliers tend to heighten customer focus, to differentiate themselves and to preserve market share. The adoption of total quality management practices across the 1980s accelerated the shifting of companies' focus onto the customer, which altered organizational structures and sales strategies and spurred widespread adoption of customer satisfaction measurement. The importance of customer satisfaction in qualification for honors such as the Malcolm Baldridge National Quality Award has fortified (and reflects) companies' dedication to measurement of satisfaction, resulting in substantial financial investment in this parameter. Research indicates that customer satisfaction assessment accounts for more than one-third of the business of leading U.S. research companies.[4]

Increased customer focus and the associated measurement of customer satisfaction have provided companies with the ability to respond to competitive pressures. Indeed, firms can achieve positive financial results through these efforts. However, a surprisingly large number of companies achieve little—or no—financial return on investments in customer satisfaction measurements.[5]

4   Shelly Reese, "Happiness Isn't Everything," *Marketing Tools*, May 1996.
5   Michael W. Lowenstein, "Keep Them Coming Back," *Marketing Tools*, May 1996.

A 1994 survey of more than 200 of the largest U.S. companies revealed:

While 92% of companies had an ongoing process for measuring and improving customer satisfaction scores...

...only 2% were able to show increases in sales or profits resulting from documented increases in customer satisfaction.

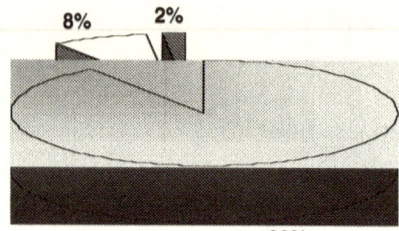

8%   2%

90%

Appendix 8: How Customer-Focused Is Your Company?

Rate how true each statement is for your company on a scale of:

1 = Very true
2 = Somewhat true
3 = Not applicable
4 = Somewhat untrue
5 = Very untrue

When you are finished, total your answers and see the interpretation on the following page.

_____	We don't know what our customers require of us.
_____	Policies exist for the convenience of the organization, not the customer.
_____	Everyone has a specialized job function and is not allowed to intrude in others' areas.
_____	Customer contact people do not have the power to make decisions.
_____	Service policies are arbitrary.
_____	We are more interested in making a profit than in building a loyal customer base.
_____	Employees are not trained in "people skills."
_____	Management does not solve problems creatively.
_____	My people don't seem to realize that customers want to be treated well.
_____	The organization is focused on solving problems rather than preventing them.
_____	We know how to handle complaints but not how to serve customers.
_____	The organization does not formally value and reward employees.

Score	Interpretation
1–11	Your organization is highly sensitized and attuned to your customers. Congratulations!
12–21	Your organization does not seem to be particularly concerned with customers.
22–60	Warning! You organization is functioning at a dangerous level of apathy concerning customers. The customers have probably already figured this out.

Appendix 9: The Nine Commandments of Being Customer-Focused

1. The customer is the most important person in the business.
2. The customer is not dependent on you. You are dependent on the customer. You work for the customer.
3. The customer is not an interruption of your work. The customer is the purpose of your work.
4. The customer does you a favor by visiting or calling your business. You are not doing customers a favor by serving them.
5. The customer is not a cold statistic. The customer is a person with feelings and emotions, just like you. Treat the customer better than you would want to be treated.
6. The customer is not someone to argue with or someone with whom to match wits.
7. The customer is as much a part of the business as anything else, including inventory, employees and your facility. If you sold the business, the customers would go with it.
8. It is your job to satisfy the needs, wants and expectations of your customers and, whenever possible, to resolve their fears and complaints.
9. The customer is the lifeblood of your business.

Appendix 10: Cost of Poor Service

To estimate how much poor service costs your company, calculate the following:

Lost Revenue	Your Cost
1. What your average customer spends in a year	_____
2. Number of customers lost each year (for average company, 20%)	_____
3. Revenue lost from lost customers (#1 x #2)	_____
4. Lost revenue from people former customers talk to (#2 x 10 people)	_____

Labor Costs	Your Cost
5. Time redoing things not done right the first time	_____
6. Time spent apologizing to customers	_____

Other Costs	Your Cost
7. Cost of shipping express instead of regular mail	_____
8. Cost of collections from angry customers who refuse to pay	_____
9. Cost of liability insurance	_____
10. Legal costs	_____
11. Telephone costs for apologizing, explaining, etc.	_____
12. Postage costs for reshipping, apologizing, explaining, etc.	_____
Total (add #3 through #12)	_____

Appendix 11: ABC Bank

Facts

- 10% of customers leave a bank each year

- 21% of the 10% leave due to poor service

- Each customer is worth $121 gross profit per year

- The cost to acquire a new customer is $150

Results for a Bank with 200,000 customers

- 20,000 customers leave (10%)

- 4,200 of those customers leave due to poor service

- Gross profit lost is: $508,200
- The cost to replace them is $630,000
- The total cost is $1,138,200!!!

Source: American Banking Association, 1990

Appendix 12: Customer Acquisition Costs

Direct
- Commissions paid
- Advertising expenses
- Marketing expenses
- Telemarketing expenses
- Salespeople's salaries, benefits, commissions, bonuses, incentives, etc.
- Reimbursements for salespeople's travel, meals, etc.
- Marketing staff's salaries, benefits, bonuses
- Telephone expenses
- Expenses for the time Management spent formulating Marketing Plan
- Secretarial and administrative assistants' salaries and benefits
- Fees paid to an advertising agency
- Cost of sales manuals and brochures, etc.

Indirect

Allocate by the applicable percentage of the company's expenses spent to support the marketing and sales staff in the following functions:

- Accounting staff
- Software engineers
- Human resources
- Salespeople's administrative support staff
- Customer service staff
- Receptionists

Overhead

Allocate the applicable percentage of operating costs spent to support the marketing, sales and non-sales support staff in the following functions:

- Rent/Mortgage
- Equipment
- Supplies
- Utilities
- Furniture
- Taxes, etc.

Appendix 13: Tips for High Customer Retention Rates

- Call each customer by name.
- Listen to what each customer has to say.
- Be concerned about each customer as an individual.
- Take sufficient time with each customer.
- Be responsive to the individual needs of each customer.
- Know your customers' preferences (recall C.J. and Andrew, first mentioned under "The Powerful Upside Potential of Customer Retention" section).
- Involve customers in your business. Ask for their advice and suggestions.
- Make customers feel important. Pay them compliments.
- Listen first to understand the customer. Then speak so they can understand you.

Appendix 14: "Moments of Truth"

What do you think are your "A" customers' "Moments of Truth" to:

A. <u>Decide to do business with your company?</u>
    1. _____
    2. _____
    3. _____

B. <u>Continue doing business with your company?</u>
    1. _____
    2. _____
    3. _____

C. <u>Stop doing business with your company?</u>
    1. _____
    2. _____
    3. _____

Appendix 15: Smart Questions

The story of Wall Street legend Warren Buffet saving the Washington, DC-based insurance company GEICO by asking smart questions is a business lesson companies should use as a model. The anecdote, described in Richard Buckingham's book, *Customer Once, Client Forever; 12 Tools for Building Lifetime Business Relationships*, tells of how Buffet saved the insurance giant when it was on the verge of bankruptcy. At the time, GEICO's stock had plummeted and analysts sounded the death knell for this once seemingly invincible company, Buckingham asserts.

Buffet, well known for his ability to save financially distressed companies, met with then-CEO James Byrne. Rather than tell him what to do, Buffet plied Byrne with questions until the wee hours of the morning so he could learn as much as possible about the distressed company. Buffet was so impressed by Byrne's answers, according to Buckingham, he purchased a huge block of GEICO stock at a low price and ultimately made a killing.

Buffet increased his fortune, but he also saved GEICO by increasing its value.

The moral of the Buffet story is that asking smart questions can be an invaluable tool for developing lifetime customers, according to Buckingham. "At the root are five umbrella questions: Who? What? When? Where? and How much?" he explains.

Here are Buckingham's 12 questions to ask regarding how to retain customers.

1. **What exactly are your needs?**
   This is a refinement of "How can we help you?" which Buckingham insists is one of the most important (yet least asked) questions. It's as basic as, "How can you serve clients effectively if you don't know exactly what they need?"

2. **When do you need the product or service?**
   Delivering superior service means knowing when customers need your products.

3. **What is your budget or price range?**
   It's basic, but it is a question that is often not asked by sales representatives. From the outset, you need to know your customers' budget so you can advise them about whether their expectations and their budget are in agreement.

4. **Who decides on the purchase and when?**
   "What good is delivering a stellar presentation in front of a person who cannot make the buying decision?" Buckingham asks.

5. **What is most important to your customer—price, quality, service or experience?**
   "What is important to you may not be important to your customer," says Buckingham.

6. **Who referred you?**
   It's important to know the origin of the referral so you can thank the person who made the referral plus learn more about any new client's needs.

7. **Are there any special conditions or concerns I should know about?**
   This is yet another basic question, leading to valuable information about best serving clients.

8. **Who else is competing for your business?**
   It may seem abrupt and inappropriate, but it's to your advantage to know who your competition is. How your customers answer this question indicates how much rapport you have built with them, according to Buckingham.

9. **What can we do to earn more of your business?**
   Find out how much business you could potentially do with a customer. Before you pursue new clients, "maximize all the business you can do with existing clients," Buckingham advises.

10. **Are you aware of all our services?**
    You'd be surprised to learn how many customers don't know the breadth of products or services companies offer.

11. **How can we develop a lifetime relationship with you?**
    Most customers will tell you.

12. **What holds you back (from doing business with us)?**
    If you believe in your business, you should have no qualms about finding out what stops customers from using your products. After investing time with prospective customers, you deserve to know what they are thinking. It's also valuable information when prospecting for new customers.

Finally, ask questions in a non-threatening manner, Buckingham advises. Questions should be a part of an easy-going, relaxed conversation. Many of us are not aware of how we ask questions. Remember: It's not an interrogation, but a conversation. Take your time. Adjust your rhythms to those of your customer so it's a comfortable exchange. Buckingham suggests writing down questions and practicing asking them. It's solid advice worth heeding.

Appendix 16: 3 Magic Questions to Ask Customers

1. What did I/we do well, that you'd like me to do again?

2. What could I/we do differently next time?

3. If you could change one thing about our organization, what would it be?

Appendix 17: Best Customer Service Companies

Annual *Fortune* Magazine Customer Satisfaction Survey
Customer Satisfaction Leaders by Industry

Industry	Company
Airlines	Southwest
Athletic Shoes	Nike
Automobiles	Mercedes-Benz
Banks	First Chicago NBD
Beverages	Coca-Cola
Beverages: Beer	Anheuser-Busch
Consumer Electronics	Zenith
Department Stores	Nordstrom
Food Processing	H.J. Heinz
Gasoline	Phillips Petroleum
Hotels	Hyatt
Household Appliances	Maytag
Insurance	State Farm
Life Insurance	New York Life Insurance
Local Telephone	BellSouth
Parcel Delivery	Federal Express
Personal Care	Colgate-Palmolive
Personal Computers	Hewlett-Packard
Restaurants	Wendy's
Sportswear	Sara Lee Apparel
Supermarkets	Publix
Telecommunications	AT&T
Utilities	Duke Power

Survey based on telephone interviews with random sample of 30,000 Americans, published in the 2/16/98 edition of Fortune *Magazine. Survey was conducted for* Fortune *by the University of Michigan business school and the American Society for Quality Control.*

Appendix 18: Resistance to Change— Moving Through It

- *Expect* resistance
- Watch the video: *"Tactics of Innovation"*
- Remember the "20-50-30 rule" (see Appendix 19)
- Explain the rationale for change
- Choose your opening moves carefully
- Provide a clear target
- Take care of the "me" issues: "What's in it for me?"
- Seek opportunities to involve your people. Have everyone involved
- Let people know there will be problems that you'll resolve together
- Over-communicate
- Reduce anxiety, rumor-mill and fears
- Beware of bureaucracy
- Wear your commitment on your sleeve
- Do what you say you will do
- Alter the reward system to support change
- Get resistance out into the open, and discuss solutions to it
- Make sure people have the know-how they need
- Track behavior and measure results
- Outrun the resisters

Appendix 19: Resistance[6]

Expect Resistance

Resistance is the most common side effect of change. If you don't encounter resistance, you have to wonder if you've really changed things much.

Here's how it works:

> Change triggers the organization's immune system. People start to resist, trying to fight off the change. It's sort of like antibodies attacking some organism that invades the body. This just seems to be the natural order of things. Upset the status quo, and here comes the opposition.
>
> Look at it this way, and you see how resistance *can* be a valuable protective device. For example, strong resistance to change might cause a company to ditch some dangerous new plan or project, in the same way your body's white blood cells fight off an infection. Resistance can protect the health of organizations as well as individuals.

But resistance also causes problems:

> Sometimes even Mother Nature screws up and misdiagnoses a situation, or tries to defend your body in ways that actually cause trouble. This happens, for example, when the excessive release of histamines causes a person to suffer from hay fever. In much the same way, an *organization's* "body chemistry" can go crazy, such that people do serious damage by resisting changes that are desperately needed.
>
> The main point here is that resistance merely offers evidence that people feel the change. Even if they put up a powerful fight against it, that in itself offers zero proof that the change is wrong. Resistance is a very reliable barometer to measure the *impact* of change. But it's not a good gauge

---

6   Excerpt taken from *RESISTANCE: Moving Beyond the Barriers to Change. A Handbook for People Who Make Things Happen.* Price Pritchett, 1996.

of how *appropriate* the change really is. You can't say change is bad medicine just because some people don't like the taste of it. You should initiate change with the idea that, more than likely, it will stir up resistance somewhere. Anticipate this, and you're better positioned to handle it.

> "Twenty percent of the people
> will be against anything."
> —*Robert Kennedy,*
> *U.S. Attorney General*

Remember the "20-50-30 Rule"

What sort of pushback is predictable when a major change program gets under way? How much resistance is "reasonable"?

If you have a reliable frame of reference, you can put things into perspective. Knowing what's "normal," you'll have a better feel for how you should react to the particular situation facing you. So let's look at the typical scenario.

We're dealing in generalities here, but the breakout usually goes about like this. Some 20% of people are "change-friendly." They're clear advocates who willingly embrace the change. You can depend on them to help drive the program. Another 50% of the folks sit on the fence. They assume a so-called neutral position, trying to figure out which way to lean. They're not necessarily hostile to change, but they're not helping like they should. The remaining 30% are the resisters. They're antagonistic toward change and often deliberately try to make it fail.

Guess which group makes the most noise? And who do you think soaks up the most time and energy from Management?

The resisters, of course. Resistance is seductive stuff. It's hard to ignore. But this is the group that gives you the least return on the efforts you invest. And giving resisters your attention often just *reinforces* their problem behavior. It's sort of like giving media attention to a small band of protesters who are demonstrating. They love it when they make the evening news, and become even more determined in defending their cause.

It makes more sense to spend your time trying to woo the fence sitters. You have far better odds of winning them over. You also should devote generous attention to the 20% who are driving the change. They deserve it the most, but ordinarily they're taken for granted. Romancing the resisters, to a large extend, is a distraction. Sure, you can put the change effort on hold, and focus on turning these people around. But how long will that take? Can you actually pull it off? And is it even essential?

Really, what you're after are *hard results,* rather than getting people to feel happy about what's going on. Never presume that you must have buy-in from everyone before you move forward. For a good percentage of people, buy-in will only come later, if at all, after the results are in which prove that the change was both appropriate and successful.

You must be willing to let squeaky wheels squeak. Save your grease for the quieter wheels that are actually carrying the load.

> "The secret of managing is to
> keep the guys who hate you
> away from the guys who are undecided."
> —*Casey Stengel*

Explain the Rationale for Change

Resistance often is rooted in a lack of understanding. People withhold support simply because they haven't figured out the situation.

Education is the first step in helping everybody get with the program. Give them the logic that's driving the change. Build your case, and make it compelling. Portray the situation as a crisis, if possible, so people come to the conclusion that *some* kind of change is absolutely necessary.

Your explanation should widen their field of vision. Relate the situation to trends in your industry. Show how your organization measures up against performance benchmarks. Try to relate the proposed changes to your organization's core values. And always consider the situation from your audience's perspective, because it needs to make sense from where *they* sit.

Granted, some people won't accept the party line. But you want everyone to understand it. *Completely.* Then at least nobody can plead ignorance. Or excuse their opposition to the change on the grounds of being uninformed. Or blame somebody else for his or her own resistant behavior.

Communicating the "why" behind change won't get rid of all resistance. Some folks will refuse to buy your logic. Some others who do accept your rationale will resist anyway because they don't like how they're affected by the change. But leaving people in the dark is just asking for trouble. Explain specifically why change is–underway—making sure your rationale holds together—and more people are likely to get on board.

Never assume everybody automatically catches on, even if the reasons for change should be obvious. Spell it out for them. And don't expect people to "get it" just because you've explained it once or twice. Some folks are slow learners—maybe they're not paying attention, or maybe they're just hard to convince.

You need to keep at it until everyone knows where the change is coming from. Without that, it's hard to hold people accountable for their behavior.

> "This taught me a lesson,
> but I'm not sure what it is."
> —*John McEnroe, on losing to Tim Mayotte*
> *in the Ebel U.S. Pro Indoor Championships*

Appendix 20: Resistance to Change

To identify barriers to change, check the problems below that you are most likely to have, and then in Part B match each with the solutions.

Part A: Why People Resist Change

_____ 1. **Loss of Control**
When people feel on top of things, change threatens them with losing control of their personal bailiwick.

_____ 2. **Uncertainty**
Predictability is comforting to many people. Change brings uncertainty, which some people find threatening.

_____ 3. **Surprise**
People like new things, but hate surprises. Sudden change is very unsettling to most of us.

_____ 4. **Habits**
People love their habits. Habits are efficient and don't require thought. Establishing new behavioral patterns is difficult.

_____ 5. **Familiarity**
The more people know things, the better they like them. (That's why companies spend a lot on advertising.) The unfamiliar is disturbing.

_____ 6. **Work**
New things usually mean more work (at least at the beginning).

_____ 7. **Competence**
People know they can do what they already do. Change means they will have to master new skills, and they don't know if they will be able to do it.

_____ 8. **Ripples**
People fear that change in one thing will lead to changes in others. (And they're right. That's the nature of a dynamic system.)

_____ 9. **Adjustment**
People are afraid it will take them a long time to adjust to any change.

Part B: Overcoming Resistance to Change

Place the numbers that you checked in Part A next to the strategies that will best fit them.

_____ Participation leads to ownership and commitment. Involve as many people as you can in the process.

_____ Communicate—clearly and often—the purpose of the change.

_____ Communicate exactly what you expect of people. Avoid surprises.

_____ Divide major change into manageable steps. (Make sure the first steps succeed.)

_____ Don't try to force people to pledge allegiance at the beginning. Let commitment grow.

_____ Be a model. Demonstrate your commitment to the change, and show your own willingness to change.

_____ Reward progress. Reinforce efforts to do things the new way.

_____ Find role models. Look for people who have already changed.

_____ Publicly commend them and let them guide others.

_____ Commit resources. Change takes time, energy and support. Make them available.

_____ Honor the past. Don't bad-mouth old ways of doing things. Allow for nostalgia, even grief. Then build excitement for the future.

Appendix 21: Six Key Observations about Paradigms[7]

1. Paradigms are common. We have them in almost all aspects of our life, whether it's professional or personal, spiritual or social.
2. Paradigms are useful. They show us what's important and what's not. They help us find important problems and then they go on to give us rules for helping to solve those problems. They focus our attention.
3. Warning: sometimes your paradigm can become **the** paradigm—the only way to do something. That is "paradigm paralysis," a terminal disease of certainty. It's easy to get, and more than a few institutions have been destroyed by it.
4. The people who create new paradigms are usually outsiders. They are not part of the established paradigm community.
5. Those practitioners of the old paradigm who choose to change to the new paradigm early in its development, "paradigm pioneers," have to be very courageous. Because, you see, the evidence provided by the new paradigm does not prove that they should be doing this.
6. Point number six is the most important: You can choose to change your rules and regulations. Human beings are not genetically coded to just one way of looking at the world. You can choose to shrug off one paradigm and adopt a new paradigm. You can choose to see the world anew.

---

7 "Discovering the Future," by Joel Barker

Appendix 22: Paradigms

1. What are the paradigms that have made your business successful?
    - Time and resources focused on sales
    -
    -
    -

2. How have they helped your business to be successful?

    - Have grown through sales
    -
    -
    -

3. What could be the downside of these paradigms?
    - Inadequate time and resources focused on training and service issues
    -
    -
    -

4. For which of these paradigms does your business have paradigm *flexibility* or paradigm *paralysis*?
    - Some paradigm flexibility
    -
    -
    -

5. Can you think of any important new information that your business might be blocking or filtering out?
    - Impact the change in banking regulations will really have on our business
    -
    -
    -

6. If in fact, many new ideas come "from the fringes," where in or outside your organization would you look to spot those ideas?
    *   Customers
    *
    *
    *

Remember:
When a paradigm shifts, everyone goes back to zero.

Appendix 23: The Ten Commandments of Customer Service[8]

1. **Ask customers what they want, and give it to them.**
   You don't define customer service. The only people who can tell you are your customers. If you want to know what they want, ask them. Ask them when you see them, ask them through surveys, ask them through focus groups, but ask them.

   But asking is not enough. Once they tell you what they want, give it to them.

2. **Rely on systems, not smiles.**
   While smiling, saying thank you, and going the extra mile are part of customer service, they are just a small part. The secret to providing good service is the creation of systems that allow you to do the job right the first time, every time. It isn't enough to treat customers fairly when they have a complaint. You must find the root cause of the problems and fix it before it affects other customers, too.

3. **Fire your customer service people.**
   You would think the best way to provide good service is to have customer service representatives. After all, what better way of taking care of your customers than by devoting a whole department to it? But that thinking, while facile, is wrong.

   Customer service is too vital a function to be left to a customer service department. Customers judge the service they receive by the contact they have with everyone at your company. And if the person who answers the

---

8   "The Ten Commandments of Customer Service" originally appeared in *StepAhead*, a publication for New England Telephone, Volume I, Issue II, June 1992. Reprinted with permission.

phone is rude or the delivery person tracks mud on their carpets, customers are going to think they have gotten poor customer service—no matter how many times you answered their calls by the third ring.

Every employee who comes into contact with customers should be empowered to solve their problems. Customer service departments impose another layer on the customer. The more people involved in solving a problem, the longer it takes to resolve.

When something goes wrong, customers don't want to deal with bureaucracies. They want to deal with one person who will take care of their problem.

4. **Fire your quality inspectors.**
   If you know someone is double-checking your work, you might not check it yourself. Those who do the work must be held accountable for it.

   The way to ensure that those people will do the job right—the first time—is to hire the best people you can find, train them well, and pay them only for the work they do correctly. If a customer has a complaint about a job, the employee who did the work initially should repair it—for free. The customer doesn't pay for the repair, and you shouldn't pay the person who had to do the work over.

5. **The answer should always be "Yes."**
   If the customer says, "Can you?" the answer should always be "Yes." Find a way to do what the customer wants. As long as his or her request is somehow related to your business, do it.

6. **There is no such thing as after-hours.**
   Somebody must always be available to handle customers' needs. Customer service is a commitment that lasts 24 hours a day. Customers will, on occasion, ask you to do something after you've closed for the day. Since the answer is always "Yes" (see Commandment number 5), it has to be "yes" then, too.

   But there's an another reason there is no such thing as after-hours. How can you provide great service if you require your customers to conform to your schedule? That has to be inconvenient for them sometimes.

That does not mean you need someone in the office 24 hours a day. There's an easier solution. Use an answering service after normal business hours. The service can then call whoever is on duty. Or record the phone messages and check them from time to time. If you really want to impress customers, give out everyone's home telephone number, or forward your business phone to your home phone.

7. **Underpromise, overdeliver.**
In other words, keep your word, and if at all possible, exceed it. For example, if you promised the job would be done by 3 PM, make sure it's completed by 2:30. If, for any reason, you can't do what you promised, let the customer know in plenty of time, and offer to make amends on the spot.

8. **Look good.**
People like to do business where they feel comfortable. Make your business look warm, clean and inviting. Take a walk around your place, trying to see things from the customer's perspective. If you aren't happy with what you see, the customers won't be either.

9. **Teach your customers how to get the best service.**
Are you always mobbed when the doors open? Suggest that customers come later in the day. Also, show your customers that if they spend a bit more time describing what's wrong, they'll have a better chance of having it quickly made right.

10. **Commit yourself to continual improvements.**
Take every single part of your operation and make it better. Set up schedules that require you to periodically reexamine every product, system and person you have. Don't end that examination without making everything a little bit better. Then once you've done it, do it again six months later, and six months after that, and...

None of this is as easy as yelling, "Lowest prices in town!" However if you implement even some of these ten commandments, you'll be well on your way to creating your own customers for life.

Appendix 24: Customer Survey—Claims

Dear Customer:

Our commitment to you includes providing superior claims service. Please assist us in monitoring and improving the quality of our claims handling by rating the service you received on your recent claim.

We survey only a select number of our customers. Your comments are very important to us. A postage-paid business reply envelope is enclosed.

The questionnaire consists of two parts: (1) Payment, and (2) Service. Please keep this in mind and report separately on each category.

Thanks very much for taking the time to respond. Your comments make a difference to us.

Sincerely,

XXX
President

Appendix 25: Customer Survey—Claims

Claims Customer Survey

Date of Claim _____ Claim Number _____
Claim _____

Payment

Did the adjustment of your claim meet your expectations? Yes _____ No _____

Service

Circle the number which best reflects your opinion. Thank you!

	Completely Satisfied	Very Satisfied	Fairly Satisfied	Somewhat Dissatisfied	Very Dissatisfied
Ease of reaching the right person to make your initial report	5	4	3	2	1
Courtesy of our representative	5	4	3	2	1
Courtesy of insurance company representative	5	4	3	2	1
Ease and efficiency of handling procedures and paperwork	5	4	3	2	1
Explanation of coverage	5	4	3	2	1
Speed of handling and payment	5	4	3	2	1
Explanation of claims process by our representative (what to expect)	5	4	3	2	1
Overall opinion	5	4	3	2	1

Your comments are welcome:

Your name is optional: _____

Appendix 26: Claims Service Guarantee

The employee-owners of XYZ Insurance pledge the following level of excellence in our claims service:

1. Calls to our office will be returned within two hours.
2. We will assist you in securing a prompt and equitable settlement in accordance with the coverages purchased.
3. We will provide guidance for you at the time your claim is reported to us. You will know what to expect.
4. Should a liability suit be initiated, we will assemble policy information and immediately notify all insurance carriers.
5. We will establish and maintain communications with you and your insurance carrier in all claims situations.
6. Based on our claims experience and knowledge, our major carriers have granted us authority to settle many claims. If your claim is within our authority, we will issue payment within 24 hours of receiving your completed claims documents.
7. For our clients who carry Workers' Compensation, disability, and business liability coverage, our advice and guidance is always readily available. In addition, we will monitor and examine premium charges, review open claims to determine their fairness and their effect on rating structure, and attempt to expedite reimbursement for claims owed to you by third party carriers.

These are promises. Please recognize that we rely on other parties to make these unique arrangements work. Carriers, appraisers, adjusters, repair shop personnel, etc. are all involved in the process. If at any time their performance is not up to your expectations, we want to know *immediately*. Our goal is to constantly demonstrate that you have made the right decision in trusting XYZ Insurance to manage your insurance program.

Appendix 27: How Don Bibeault Uses the Old 80/20 Formula In Business Turnarounds—You Can, Too![9]

How It Works

I help clients identify the 20% of their businesses that matters most—20% of customers, 20% of products, 20% of the sales force. I then help them derive even *more* business from that top tier.

That simple strategy is essential in the turnaround situation where costs must be cut in total, while redeploying greater support to the core customers that generate the bulk of your business. But any business—no matter how successful—can become more effective and more profitable by focusing on its top 20%.

The 80/20 rule isn't always self-evident. In an industrial company with which I recently worked, only 56% of sales came from the top 20% of customers. But when I looked more deeply, I found that 91% of *profits* came from that top 20%.

In many troubled companies, 100% of profits comes from the top 20% of customers. These companies got into trouble because they lost money on 80% of their customers—a financial burden for which the top 20% could not compensate, despite their superior value to the company.

Vital Lesson: Most businesses spend too much effort satisfying customers, or selling products, that make little or no contribution to the bottom line.

Reality: By cutting back, you really do make the business much more efficient. Refocusing your efforts on your top customers and your top products does pay.

---

9   *Bottom Line* Business, Volume 27, Number 5.

Identifying the Top 20%

Very few businesses have trouble identifying the 20% of customers who generate 80% of the revenue. The problem is they are not always the customers who are generating 80% of profitability.

Don't focus only on sales. You also must look at what it costs to generate those sales. You may have a customer who buys a lot, but is so demanding that the cost of satisfying those special needs eats up every penny of the profits. To make the 80/20-rule work, you must develop systems that assess the profitability of each customer.

Accurate profit analysis of this kind requires a degree of guesswork about allocating direct and indirect costs. Get the company's accounting people to assist in this exercise. It doesn't have to be complicated. You can come close by checking daily time sheets for two months to find out how much time you're actually spending on each customer. With that information in hand, you can make some crude assumptions about the allocation of overhead.

Implementing an 80/20 Strategy

Once you've identified the critical few customers who are most profitable, you can begin cutting off the customers who aren't so profitable.

The cutoff point can vary from one business to the next, which is why your measurement should be relative and not absolute. It may be that in your business even the bottom 20% is still profitable, while another business might be losing money on the bottom 20%, 40% or even 60% of customers.

But, even in a case like this, it may not be necessary to abruptly cut of all unprofitable or marginally profitable customers.

Other approaches you can try…

- **Increasing revenue from the marginal customers.** That's what banks do with below-top-tier customers. They charge service fees on checking accounts with small balances. Because customers with small balances eat up a lot of teller time, some banks charge up to $3 for each visit to a teller.
- **Reducing the delivery cost of service to these customers.** We studied one company in which people who delivered on-site service to customers were spending 60% of their time with customers who generated only 5% of sales.

Response: The bottom 20% of customers were simply eliminated. The next 40% stopped receiving on-site service. Instead, they were given an 800 number that connected them to technicians. The idea worked so well that within six months, even top-tier customers were demanding the same 800-number service. In the end, the company was able to limit on-site service to only a few big customers. The rest went to the 800 number.

Traps to Avoid

In addition to finding creative ways to improve the value of marginal customers, there are several costly traps to beware of when implementing an 80/20 strategy:

- **Avoid inadvertently "killing" your next great customer.** Don't just do a computer run and automatically mail out notices to the bottom echelons of customers saying, "We don't want to do business with you." Qualify your research. Is a customer in the bottom 20% because it is still a new customer? Could it have the *potential* to grow much bigger?

  To make shrewd decisions, get direct input from sales reps, customer service reps and others who know the customers, and who can make sure a new customer that has potential isn't cut off along with a mature customer that will never make a profit for you.

- **Pace your cutbacks.** Once you cut your customer base back to the top 20%, you might be tempted to do another 80/20 screen on that top 20%…and then another on the remaining top 20%. But beware—keep doing that and you could literally tear your business apart.

Better: Do your 80/20 on a regular basis—but never more than once a year. Avoid the temptation of doing 80/20 screens on a monthly, or even a quarterly, basis.

At the beginning, an 80/20 policy can produce a temporary slowdown for the business. Keep an extra-close watch on costs during this year so any slowdown in revenues is matched by reduced spending.

The key to an 80/20 policy is the redeployment of resources away from the marginal many and to the critical few that account for current profits and future growth.

Appendix 28: The Five Prerequisites to Tiered Service Success[10]

Tiered service is one of the many aspects of retention that can do wonders for revenues, if properly handled—but if poorly handled, watch out! The potential benefits of tailoring service to customers based on their actual or potential profitability to the organization are so great, however, we are constantly on the lookout for research and case studies on how (and how not) to proceed.

TARP study offers insights on benefits and strategies.

In the spirit of learning more about tiered benefits, we were pleased to attend the SOCAP Symposium session in New York City in March of 2002, "Tiered Service: Marketing Nirvana or Road to Disaster? Path to Profit or Road to Ruin?" While the title may not be the most succinct we've come across in our travels, the presentation, led by Cynthia Grimm of TARP, contained a wealth of information and insight on the topic.

Why tiered service is worth it—despite the risks.

Noting that tiered/segmented service has been growing over the past few years, Grimm offered one good reason. 83% of those businesses that successfully implemented a tiered service program saw their revenues increase, according to a 2001 study, *Factors Leading to Successful Tiered/Segmented Service*, by TARP research through the Center for Customer Experience Leadership (CCEL).

Of course, horror stories abound about tiered service strategies gone wrong. As has been reported in *ICRM* and elsewhere, bad tiered service strategies can have dire consequences for companies. These include:

---

10   *IOMA's Report on Customer Relationship Management*, June, 2002

1.   **Inflated customer expectations.** That's why managing customer expectations has been a hot topic in retention, customer relationship management and customer service conferences for ages.

2.   **Alienation of mid-level customers.** As *ICRM* has noted before, these customers can sometimes be your most profitable because you give them fewer perks than their more precious counterparts.

3.   **Elite customers getting poor service from different departments of the business.** "The whole silo thing," Grimm explained. She offered the case of a bank that discovered 50% of its top-shelf customers were planning to leave because, although they were catered to by their "personal bankers," they weren't treated well when they visited different branches.

4.   **Over-marketing to top customers.** Grimm told of one business that realized, to its horror, that it had been sending 200 offers a *year* to its premier customers.

5.   **Representatives' frustration.** If company representatives don't understand it, they can see tiered service as unfair and not deliver it, warned Grimm.

6.   **Increasing service costs without seeing sufficient increases in revenues.** Tiered service may increase revenues, but it also can do quite a bit to enlarge expenses.

This is only a short list of the ways tiered service can be improperly foisted on the marketplace. In the sidebar, "How to Sabotage Tiered Service," *ICRM* offers one of our favorite cautionary tales on this topic, courtesy of the crm-forum.com Web site.

Setting the stage for tiered service success. Your organization needn't be the subject of a cautionary tale or two of its own, asserts Grimm. In her presentation, she offered what she termed "five prerequisites for tiered service success" that we believe can help you avoid some of the more onerous and embarrassing tiered service mistakes.

An overview:

> *Prerequisite one:* **Define clear, simple objectives.** For starters, Grimm offered three "musts" for any company's tiered service strategy:
>
> 1. Address the value and costs for each segment.
> 2. Clearly define the specific benefits for each segment ("be careful about bleeding across segments," she cautions).

3. Define three to four tiers, at the most. Grimm reported hearing of organizations with six or seven tiers. Needless to say, things "got a little mushy after a while."

As for objectives, Grimm suggested the following:

1. Enhance the loyalty of existing top-tier customers (this is the most common objective cited by the CCEL study respondents).
2. Attract new high-value customers by offering new benefits.
3. Make money by providing enhanced service for a fee (perhaps one of the least common objectives for tiers).
4. Reduce the costs of servicing lower-tier customers. "Be careful! That's the objective that gets most companies into trouble," according to Grimm.

Prerequisite two: **Ensure effective internal buy-in and infrastructure.** You must, of course, get senior management, sales, and service representatives on board. And there's one more must, Grimm observed: According to the top 10% to 20% of companies who reported the highest revenue gains from their tiered service implementations (a.k.a., the "success group"), sales and operations/customer service should share the implementation load.

Beyond buy-in and cooperation, another element of this prerequisite is the technology infrastructure necessary to identify the status of customers and to track their purchase and service history. Last but not least, front-line staff need training and response guidelines.

Prerequisite three: **Set proper expectations.** The worst time to modify customer expectations is at the time of service, but it's also true that getting sales people to set proper expectations with customers at the time of sale—the best time to do so, says Grimm—is like asking pigs to fly. *Inflating* expectations seems more up their alley, and that's a tough habit to break. Nonetheless, you should try to inform customers sooner rather than later. Grimm offered research from Mannington Floors that showed the wonderful effects of its providing customers with care and warranty information up front. These customers:

1. Were 10% to 30% more satisfied
2. Were more likely to buy again (60% of customers who received information "definitely would buy" versus only 35% of those who didn't)

3. Had fewer problems: 23% of those informed reported problems vs. 41% of uninformed customers
4. Were less at risk due to problems (6.9% of informed customers vs. 12.9% of uninformed)
5. Complained 18% more often when they were unhappy, **but** were 26% happier with the outcome (a rather mixed blessing)

Prerequisite four: **Provide easy access for all levels.** Make sure you offer a broad range of hours for customers who need to talk, and acceptable levels of access for *all* customers.

Prerequisite five: **Ensure effective follow-through and follow up.** This is a familiar "key to success" if ever there was one. Grimm mentioned the following specifics:

1. Make sure you have internal service agreements and processes in place that build confidence that promises made by front-line representatives will be kept.
2. Establish survey mechanisms to evaluate the impact of your tiered service strategy for each customer segment (1) by type of transaction and (2) across the customer lifecycle, including pre-purchase.

Conclusion: Tiered service can work for you, as long as you put the requisite time and effort into preparing for, implementing, and executing your plan. If you're looking for a quick CRM-related fix, this isn't it, but if you have the time to do it right, tiered service can do wonders for your bottom line.

Appendix 29: Service Standards

	Service Standards	A	B	C
	(number of days or hours refers to business days or hours)			
1	# Hours for a Phone Call to be Returned	4	8	24
2	# Hours before Written Correspondence will be Acknowledged (mail/fax)	8	16	32
3	# Days for Claims to be Submitted to Insurance Company	1	1	1
4	# Days for Certificates to be Mailed (requests to fax or if customer is here to pick up—must be done as requested)	1	2	3
5	# Days for Billing Inquiries to be Answered (B and C accounts will be given the toll-free number to call the insurance company)	1	3	5
6	# Days for Change Requests to be Submitted to the Company With Copy to the Insured (if no binding authority with the company, change to be processed and mailed/faxed that day)	2	2	2
7	# Days for New Policies to be Confirmed for Customers With Binders	1	2	3
8	Account Executive to Call Contact at Insured Prior to Going on Vacation	Yes	No	No
9	Minimum # Contacts With Producer on Account During Policy Term (other than renewal process)	2	1	0
10	Special Pay Plans for Customers (must be approved by management)	Yes	No	No
11	Schedule of Payments For Customers	Yes	No	No
12	In-Person Delivery of Policies	Yes	Maybe	No
13	# Days Prior to Renewal Date that Renewal Quote Is Given to Insured	20	10	5
14	# Days Prior to Renewal Date that Binders are Given to Insured	10	5	1
15	Contact on Late Pay Notices From Companies on Direct Billed Items	Yes	No	No

16	# Times We Will Rewrite a Policy Cancelled For Nonpayment During Policy Term	1	1	0
17	Account Executive Will Visit Client at Least Once Annually	Yes	No	No

Appendix 30: Standards of Performance

Our customer service, accounting, and claims teams are concerned about your success, and we have a program to help you achieve your goals. As professionals, we are committed to providing quality service, and have set "Standards of Performance" for your benefit. The following is an outline of service standards you may expect from us:

1. Your phone call will be returned within three business hours. Immediate assistance is always available during business hours on request.
2. Your written correspondence will be answered within five business days.
3. Your claims will be submitted to the insurance company within one business day.
4. Your certificates of insurance will be mailed within two business days of your request with a copy sent to you. Same day service is available whenever necessary upon request.
5. Your accounting inquiries will be answered within three business days.
6. Your requests for changes in coverage will be submitted to insurance companies within two business days with a copy sent to you.
7. Your new policies will be confirmed by written binders sent to you within three business days.
8. Your renewal policies will be confirmed by written binders sent to you 20 days prior to your renewal date, or a written status report will be provided.

Appendix 31: "Wow!"ing "A" Customers

What have you done to "Wow!" your "A" customers?

1. _____
2. _____
3. _____
4. _____
5. _____
6. _____
7. _____
8. _____
9. _____
10. _____

Appendix 32: Increasing the Value of Your Customer Base

1. How effective are you at prospecting for "A" customers?

   Ineffective 1 2 3 4 5 6 7 8 9 10 Very Effective

2. How effective are you at keeping your "A" customers very satisfied?

   Ineffective 1 2 3 4 5 6 7 8 9 10 Very Effective

3. How effective are you at upgrading your "B" customers into "A" customers?

   Ineffective 1 2 3 4 5 6 7 8 9 10 Very Effective

4. How effective are you at growing "C" customers into "B" customers?

   Ineffective 1 2 3 4 5 6 7 8 9 10 Very Effective

5. How effective are you at phasing out your "C" customers that can't be upgraded to "B"s or "A"s?

   Ineffective 1 2 3 4 5 6 7 8 9 10 Very Effective

Appendix 33: Rework

"Fixing costs" are expenses for doing things over that were not done right the first time. The following events may result from not doing things right the first time. Check the items that apply to your company and ask your accounting department to calculate costs (such as time, overhead and materials):

_____	Doing work over
_____	Wasted material and scrap
_____	Handling complaints
_____	Rewriting manuals and procedures
_____	Redesigning forms
_____	Overtime to fix things
_____	Underbilling
_____	Customers paying incorrect bills late
_____	Premium shipping and express delivery
_____	Sales not closed due to lack of follow-up
_____	Liability insurance and claims
_____	Down time
_____	Extra time spent with suppliers
_____	Lack of clarity on your part that induces customer errors
_____	Reentering data
_____	Your service costs (legal, telephone, postage)
_____	Other _____

Appendix 34: Economics of Customer Retention

If you are working with a group, divide the questions below among yourselves. Discuss individual questions in a small group, then meet back together as a whole. Be prepared to present your answers and explain your rationales. Be as specific as possible.

1. What is the economic value of a customer?

2. How much does it cost you to acquire a customer?

3. How much does it cost you to retain a customer?

4. How much does it cost you to regain a lost customer?

5. Why is it critical to your company to know the answer to these questions?

Appendix 35: Quantifying the Customer Retention vs. Profitability Link[11]

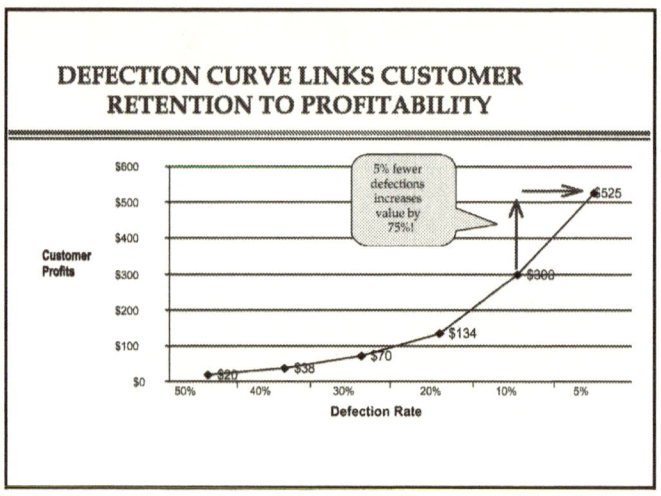

DEFECTION CURVE LINKS CUSTOMER RETENTION TO PROFITABILITY

By comparing the net present value of customer lifecycle profit streams at the current defection rate with the net present value of profit streams at lower defections rates, a company may calculate the increase in profit generated from increasing customer retention. This graph provides a sample defection curve, which correlates customer profits to customer retention.

The example above shows that if this particular company cuts its defection rate from 20% to 10%, the average lifetime of the customer doubles from five to ten years, and the value of that customer more than doubles—jumping from $134 to $300. As the defection rate decreases another 5%, the average life-time doubles again and profits rise by 75%, from $300 to $525.

---

11 "Zero Defections: Quality Comes to Services," Frederick Reichheld and Earl Sasser, Harvard Business Review, 1990.

According to Reichheld and Sasser, "Knowing that defections are closely linked to profitability helps explain why some companies with loyal, long-time customers can outperform competitors with lower unit costs and high market share but high customer churn."

Appendix 36: A Common Friend Thought We Should Meet[12]

                                                    date

—-

—-

—-

—-

Dear—:

Dan Verrico, of Retirement Concepts and Worcester Chamber of Commerce, suggested that you and I meet.

Quite honestly, neither one of us knows if there is a fit between your business' needs and our unique and proven Customer Loyalty and Retention services. Dan felt that it was highly likely that you would benefit greatly from our services.

My office will call you within the next few weeks to determine if you have an interest in learning more about our unique programs.

I look forward to meeting your personally.

Very truly yours,

XXX
President

---

12 This letter is courtesy of Roger Sitkins.

Appendix 37: Cross-Selling Bonus Plan

PURPOSE

Growing value for shareholders, clients, and employee-owners by capturing more of the insurance business of individual and commercial policyholders. Converting policyholders into multi-line clients and thereby increasing customer retention.

EXPECTATION

Fostering employee teamwork and stimulating successful referrals (i.e. written business).

REFERRALS COVERED BY PLAN

An employee-to-employee personal introduction (by telephone or in person) of a current policyholder for additional coverage, or a policyholder with another agency.

REFERRALS ARE TO BE DIRECTED TO

Producer of record for:
Commercial   _____
Personal   _____
Employee Benefits   _____
Life   _____

POLICIES ELIGIBLE FOR CROSS-SELLING BONUS

All except individual health.

BEGINNING DATE

Friday, October 3, 2003

INCENTIVE

$5 per name referred

PAYMENT OF BONUS

Honor system, using "Cross-Selling Referral Record." Paid monthly (with usual 30-day lag) as part of regular paycheck.

EDUCATION AND TRAINING

To be scheduled with designated person, to demonstrate ways to diplomatically cross-sell. For example: "How about a milk shake (auto) with that burger (homeowners) and fries (life insurance)?

Appendix 38: Debriefing Meetings

A. Have a debriefing meeting after a sales presentation to an "A" or "B" prospect regardless of its success. You want to know why the prospect decided as s/he did. This will help to narrow down the factors that are contributing to the company's success and their loses, and increase the sales-hit ratio for the company.

   1. Establish this debriefing conversation/meeting at the beginning of the presentation. "We would like to tell you about our debriefing process. After sales presentations, we will have someone who is not part of this presentation call you and ask how you made your decision. It is one method that we use to constantly improve. Will that work for you?"

B. Have a debriefing meeting annually with "A" and "B" clients, and again whenever a client leaves. The annual meeting is designed to uncover what is working and what is not. These individuals have valuable data that will immeasurably assist the company in increasing its sales-hit ratio and retention rates.

C. Have debriefing meetings after any major purchase, cross-sale, referral or other significant event.

Appendix 39: Testimonial Form

In the book, *Awakening the Corporate Soul,* authors John Izzo and Eric Klein describe how Medtronic, a medical electronic equipment company, reminds employees of how important their work is.

Once a year, executives at the Minneapolis-based company invite former patients to visit the firm and tell employees how Medtronic equipment saved or improved their lives. After just one or two patient testimonials, employees are reaching for their handkerchiefs. These dramatic life and-death stories clearly remind employees that they are not just selling machines—they are saving lives.

The following is an example of a form that can be used to solicit testimonials from customers.

> **Please take a moment to list all the always our products and services have helped to improve your life.**

1. _____
2. _____
3. _____
4. _____
5. _____
6. _____
7. _____
8. _____
9. _____
10. _____

Appendix 40: Unique Selling Proposition

❑ Your Unique Selling Proposition (U.S.P.) consists of your competitive advantages. These are the unique and appealing ideas and activities that separate you from all the other "me, too" competitors.

❑ The U.S.P. answers the question every prospect (and client) asks him-or herself: "Why should I buy (renew) my insurance with you?"

❑ The U.S.P. explains why it would irrational **not** to buy insurance from you!

List the five things that make your company truly unique:

1. _____
2. _____
3. _____
4. _____
5. _____

Appendix 41: Client "To Do" List

		Weekly	Monthly	Quarterly	Yearly
1	Sales meeting	X			
2	Debrief lost sales	X			
3	Low risk practice	X			
4	"A" rehearse prior	X			
5	Celebrate	X			
6	Closure reports		X		
7	Top 20 Prospect List		X		
8	Top 20 "A" Clients List		X		
9	Client relationship management		X		
10	Referral review		X		
11	Top Five Centers of Influence			X	
12	Trade down bottom 5%				X
13	Performance Agreements—CSRs & Producers				X
14	Goals				X
15	Producer P/L				X
16	USP/UCA				X
17	Staff survey			X	

Appendix 42: Employee Retention: Perks you CAN Afford[13]

Once a quarter, Mark Firmani closes his company for the day and takes his seven employees to the movies. It isn't that business is slow. Firmani, president of Firmani and Associates, a public-relations firm in Seattle, says that the $500,000 company has plenty of work. Just the same, four times a year the employees don their pagers, forward the phones to the voice-mail system, and take in a matinee.

Firmani claims he shuts down for the day to stay competitive—competitive in the market for good employees, that is. Seattle is, after all, Microsoft country, and the local economic boom has attracted some big-name public-relations players to the area. "There are agencies here that can charge big bucks and pay well above the national scale," says Firmani. "So I try to give this place a more enjoyable atmosphere." He has also found that when Microsoft and others raise the employee-benefits bar, he must follow their lead. Microsoft has company-subsidized cafeterias. So Firmani provides weekly catered lunches as well as daily supplies of soda, juice and candy.

Your business may not be in Seattle, but you still face the same challenge as Firmani: making your company a more attractive place to work. With national unemployment extremely low, it's harder than ever to hold on to good employees. According to Matt Weinstein, author of *Managing to Have Fun*, these days companies—especially those in high-tech industries—almost have to treat their employees as volunteers. "Employees know they could work anywhere," says Weinstein. "So companies need to create an environment where people feel appreciated and recognized." When it comes to employee retention, big companies can throw money at the problem. Chances are, you can't. That's why smart entrepreneurs are looking for low-cost

---

13 *Inc.*, November 1997.

ways to add zing to their benefits packages. Consider some of these possibilities:

Give flexibility, for some employees, flexible schedules can be a valued perk. David Kaufer, co-founder of Kaufer Miller Communications, a 27-person communications agency in the Seattle area, had an employee who was distressed about his long commute. Kaufer and the employee worked out a schedule that included four ten-hour workdays, with Fridays off, until the worker could find a closer residence. "He really appreciates the three hours a day he doesn't have to spend on I-5," says Kaufer. Kaufer also set another employee up with a home office, so she could move closer to her fiancée in southern Washington.

Even manufacturers can offer scheduling options, albeit within limits. At Autumn Harp, a 65-person manufacturer of skin-care prod-

ucts in Bristol, Vermont, founder Kevin Harper gives many employees the option to work one day a week at home. About 10% of his 65 employees take him up the offer. Harper admits, though, that for certain positions, working at home is not feasible. "Production workers can't bring their machine home," he explains.

What could cost less—and offer more flexibility—than a casual dress code? At Half Price Books, a $56-million chain of discount bookstores that has its

headquarters in Dallas, president Sharon Anderson Wright just asks that her employees wear clothing that is clean, not torn, and free of offensive slogans or graphics. "After a big debate, we decided they had to wear shoes," she says.

Firmani, too, is sartorially permissive. His PR professionals usually wear jeans, sometimes sweats. All Firmani requires is that employees be within 15 minutes of wearing something presentable in case a client drops by. "I keep a suit here at he office," says Firmani. "Not that I wear it much."

Share the perks of your business. Is there an aspect of your business that you could turn into an inexpensive employee benefit? Orval Masive, CEO of Hot Topic, a $44-million chain of music-related-apparel and accessories stores based in Pomona, California, reimburses employees for tickets to rock concerts. The business tie-in? For Hot Topic, the shows provide important market research. To qualify for the reimbursement, employees must return with a report on the fashions that the band and the fans were wearing, and with other merchandising ideas.

Why not let employees share in perks you provide to your clients? Rick Born, CEO of Born Information Services, a $36-million information-technology consulting firm headquartered in Minneapolis, already was paying to entertain customers at a skybox at a local arena. Now Born splits use of the skybox between clients and employees.

Do fun stuff. CEOs and employees alike need way to blow off steam. David Kaufer periodically rents a bus and—without advance notice—takes his staff to a Mariners game or to play laser tag. (One caveat: keep mystery events non-threatening. Firmani once took his staff on a surprise outing to go parasailing, a form of parachuting that involves being air lifted by a boat. He watched one evidently frightened staff member

turn increasingly white awaiting his turn. "I felt horrible," says Firmani)

Some companies offer travel, such as a cruise to the Bahamas, to salespeople, or even to the entire staff if sales or profit goals are met. For a few years, Rick Born offered such a trip. The perk was popular but logistically difficult and expensive. Also, some workers couldn't go because they couldn't arrange baby-sitting. So Born decided to take the money he was spending on trips and invest it in lakefront property in a Minnesota resort area. Staffers now take turns bringing their families to one of the six company-owned houses—a benefit that's admittedly not cheap. But Born says that he was spending the money anyway, and this away he's building equity through mortgage payments.

Feed employees' bodies. And their souls. The easiest way to an employee's heart?

Through the proverbial stomach. That's

why Jack Schacht, president of National Trade Association (NTA), in Glenview, Illinois, provides monthly in-house luncheons for the company's 50 employees. He finds that the luncheons promote camaraderie and offer a chance to celebrate birthdays at the commercial barter company.

Mark Zweig of Zweig White & Associates, a $3.1-million consulting and publishing firm in Natick, Massachusetts, goes even further and provides his 37 employees with free food and drink all day every day. "Our people work long hours," says Zweig. "We want to make it easier for them to do so."

In the soul department, Autumn Harp gives employees two days a year paid community-service time. Employees have used the time to volunteer at local schools, paint a nearby teen homeless shelter, and rebuild an AIDS clinic damaged by arson.

In addition, Autumn Harp offers employees not only a health plan but also a "wellness reimbursement" of $200 a year for anything related to their "mental, physical, or spiritual well-being." Past reimbursement items have ranged from gym memberships to scuba lessons. One employee even put the money toward house paint, arguing that it would make him feel good.

Offer advancement opportunities. One of the best incentives for ambitious people is opportunity. Sharon Anderson Wright of Half Price Books fills management positions by promoting from within, ensuring that long-term employees have a chance to rise—and that new employees have an incentive to stay. "It's dancing with the ones that brought you," says Wright. Firmani provides a well-defined career track, with specific criteria for raises and advancement. For example, employees that bill 1,200 hours a year and make two new-business contacts know exactly how much their salaries will increase as a result.

Pat people on the back. Few perks are cheaper, easier, or more effective than recognition, and it can take a variety of forms. At Command Software, an anti-virus-software company in Jupiter, Florida, Dyan Dyer created an "Angel of the Month" award that recognizes "random acts of kindness" within the company. One recent winner: an employee who volunteered to house a programmer the company had brought over from Germany, help him get acclimated and help him find an apartment. That winner received a gift certificate for a local spa, plus a small porcelain angel for her desk.

Far greater than the cost of the mostly modest investments is the value of the employee loyalty you can get in return. For example, Rick Born claims his turnover rate is one-third his industry's average—and he credits the difference to the perks he offers, especially the company-owned vacation homes. "I have employees' kids say to me, 'Thank you, Mr. Born, for letting us go to your cabin,'" he says. "You'd never get that from a kid if you gave his dad a $5,000 dollar raise. I had one guy say, 'I couldn't leave if I wanted to; my family would divorce me.'"

Resources:

1,001 Ways to Reward Employees by Bob Nelson, *301 Ways to Have Fun at Work* by Dave Hemsath and Leslie Yerkes, *Managing to Have Fun* by Matt Weinstein.

Appendix 43: Old vs. New Realities Work Environment

Old Realities	New Realities
Blame	Responsibility
Information-Poor Environment	Information-Rich Environment
Fear of Mistakes	Love of Job
Territoriality	Cooperation
Suspicion	Trust
Protectiveness	Sharing
Lying	Truth
Cover-Ups	Openness
Avoidance of Risk	Risk-taking
Low Morale	High Morale
Absenteeism	High Attendance
Low Productivity	High Productivity
High Turnover	Low Turnover
Low Loyalty	High Loyalty
Job	Balance of Life/ Growth Opportunities
Employee/Employer	Partnership
Top Down	Ask Employees
On-the-Job Training	Continuous Training

Appendix 44: Customer/Employee Relationship Mirror

Customer relations mirror employee relations. The way you treat your employees is the way they will treat your customers. Let's take a look:

Organization to Employee	*Employee to Customer*
What are your problems and how we can help solve them?	How may I help you?
We want you to know what is happening in our business.	I can help you because I know what's going on.
We're all part of the business, so we're all responsible for what happens here.	I have the authority to help you, and I'm proud of my ability to do so.
We treat each other with professional respect.	I value you as an individual.
We stand behind each other's decisions and support each other.	You can count on me, and on my company, to deliver on our promises.

Appendix 45: Your Company's Customer/Employee Mirror

Analyze your company's typical messages to determine what employees mirror to customers. Then develop new, changed messages where needed:

Message to Employees	Translation to Customers	Changed Message

Appendix 46: Your Word Choice with Co-Workers Makes a Difference

Call attention to people's mistakes indirectly

Fight Starters
You didn't do it right.

Communication Beginings
There are a few more areas that need to be completed.

Use "I" messages

Fight Starters
You're wrong.

Communication Beginnings
I can see there's been a miscommunication/misunderstanding.

You're confusing me.

I'm confused.

Avoid giving orders

Fight Starters
You have to…

Communication Beginnings
It will be better if we…

You should have done it this way

We want your next visit to go as smoothly as possible. This will assist you next time…Will you please…

Take responsibility

Fight Starters
I can't…

Communication Beginnings
I don't have the….However,…should be able to help you.

It's not my fault/job.

Let me see what I can do to help.

Avoid causing defensiveness

Fight Starters	*Communication Beginnings*
You never do it right.	This is…is not done correctly.
You're always late.	You…come in late.
You filled this out okay, But…	You filled this out well,…
What's your problem?	Please tell me what happened.

Appendix 47: Who You Are Makes A Difference

A teacher in New York decided to honor each of his seniors in high school by telling them the difference they each made. Using a process developed by Helice Bridges of Del Mar, California, he called each student to the front of the class, one at a time.

First, he told them how the student made a difference to him and the class. Then, he presented each of them with a blue ribbon imprinted in gold letters with, "Who I am makes a difference."

Afterwards, the teacher decided to do a class project to see what kind of impact recognition would have on a community. He gave each of the students three more ribbons and instructed them to go out and spread this acknowledgment ceremony. Then, they were to follow-up on the results and report back to the class.

One of the boys in the class went to a junior executive in a nearby company and honored the executive for helping him with his career planning. He gave the man a blue ribbon and put it on his shirt. Then, he gave him two extra ribbons, and said, "We're doing a class project on recognition. We'd like you to go out, find somebody to honor, and give that person a blue ribbon. Then, give the person the extra blue ribbon so he or she can acknowledge a third person to keep this acknowledgment ceremony going. Then, please report back to me and tell me what happened."

Later that day, the junior executive went in to see his boss, who had been noted, by the way, as being kind of a grouchy fellow. He sat his boss down and he told him that he deeply admired him for being a creative genius. The boss seemed very surprised. The junior executive asked him if he would accept the gift of the blue ribbon and would he give the executive permission to put it on him. His surprised boss said, "Well, sure." The junior executive took the blue ribbon and placed it right on his boss's jacket above his heart. As he gave him the last extra ribbon, he said, "Would you do me a favor? Would you take this extra ribbon and pass it on by honoring somebody else? The young boy who first gave me the ribbons is doing a project in school and we want to keep this recognition ceremony going and find out how it affects people."

That night, the boss came home to his 14-year-old son and sat him down. He said, "The most incredible thing happened to me today. I was in my office and one of the junior executives came in and told me he admired me and gave me a blue ribbon for being a creative genius. Imagine! He thinks I'm a creative genius! Then, he put this blue ribbon that says 'Who I am makes a difference' on my jacket above my heart. He gave me an extra ribbon and asked me to find somebody else to honor.

"As I was driving home tonight, I started thinking about whom I would honor with this ribbon and I thought about you. I want to honor you. My days are really hectic and when I come home I don't pay a lot of attention to you. Sometimes I scream at you for not getting good enough grades in school and for your bedroom being a mess, but somehow, tonight, I just wanted to sit here and, well, just let you know that you do make a difference to me. Besides your mother, you are the most important person in my life. You're a great kid and I love you!"

The startled boy started to sob and sob, and he couldn't stop crying. His whole body shook. He looked up at his father and said through his tears, "I was planning to commit suicide tomorrow, Dad, because I didn't think you loved me. Now I don't need to."

Who I am makes a difference because I am a person with a heart and feelings and a need to be accepted. Some days I feel the way this boy does and I just need to be acknowledged.

If you know anyone who means a lot to you, I encourage you to let that person know. You never know what kind of difference a little encouragement can make to a person. Tell it to all of the people who mean anything to you, or tell it to the one or two people who mean the most.

Remember that you deserve a blue ribbon! Who you are makes a difference! Pass it on!

Appendix 48: Stress Busters

1. Breathe deeply and slowly for a few minutes.

2. Listen to music that relaxes or energizes you.

3. Visualize yourself in a pleasant scene from your past—a favorite vacation spot, etc.

4. Have a good laugh. Keep cartoons at your desk, or think about something that makes you laugh.

5. Take a stretch break.

6. Go for a walk or look out the window for a few minutes.

7. Ask yourself what is the worst thing that could happen if you make a mistake, miss a deadline, etc.?

8. Do something nice for yourself when you complete a difficult task.

9. Meditate.

10. Get a massage, or give yourself one, i.e., a foot massage.

11. Exercise regularly and get plenty of sleep.

12. Spend time with family or friends.

13. Delegate responsibility wherever possible.

14. Spend time volunteering for a cause you believe in.

15. Change your focus. Concentrate on something else for five minutes.

16. Take time out to play. Those who take time out to play are healthier and happier on the job.

17. Pamper yourself when possible and when within your budget.

18. Worry only about the things you can control.

19. Eat a healthy diet.

20. Take good care of yourself and your health.

21. Set realistic goals.

22. Hug someone—it does a lot to calm you down.

23. Take a long hot bath after a difficult day.

24. Take a shopping break. Buy something for yourself or for someone else.

25. Make a list of all the things that make you happy. Refer to the list when you need to reduce your stress, and choose to experience something from your list.

26. co-worker.

27. Do a routine task. This can be a soothing diversion.

28. Set priorities. List all the things you must do, and do them in order of importance.

29. Take a relaxation break. Pull back from your desk and concentrate on relaxing all of your muscles one at a time.

30. As a last resort, take steps necessary to change your situation.

Appendix 49: "Wow!"ing Employees

What have you done to "Wow!" your employees?

1. _____
2. _____
3. _____
4. _____
5. _____
6. _____
7. _____

Appendix 50: Complaints and Employee Empowerment

There is little question that empowering people who serve customers improves your customers' view of your service quality. Statistics show that empowerment actually saves money. Let's look at an example:

Let's say the average cost to issue full credit on a complaint is $50. Let's also say that it costs about $25 to investigate a complaint before issuing credit, and that in two-thirds of the cases, you'll issue a full credit after investigating. Here's what the numbers would look like:

Pay off one complaint   total: $50.00

Investigate one complaint ($25.00) and
pay off $2/3$ of complaints ($50 x $2/3$ = $33.33)   total: $58.33

The average cost of investigating and resolving one complaint is $58.33. Thus, you actually save the company $8 each time if you empower subordinates to pay off small complaints. Also, since most customers really are honest, you'll gain many times the value of the $50 in goodwill and reputation by settling on the spot.

Furthermore, research shows that if you do solve a customer's problem without haggling, more than 90% will forget the problem and continue to do business with the company. However, if their problems have to be referred to managers and then take days or weeks to resolve, only 70% of customers will stay with the company.

Appendix 51: Forbidden Phrases

Key: When a customer calls, she/he wants something done. She/he does not want to know what you cannot do. **Always** emphasize what you **can** do.

Here are some phrases to avoid and some suggested alternatives.

1. *When placing a customer on hold, ask permission first, and let him/her know for how long:*

Forbidden Phrase	What to Say Instead
"Hang on a second; I will be right back."	"It may take me two or three minutes to get that. Are you able to hold?"

2. *Never use "policy" as a reason for not doing something:*

Forbidden Phrase	What to Say Instead
"The policy is…"	Explain the reasoning behind the policy.

3. *"No" when used at the beginning of a sentence:*

Forbidden Phrase	What to Say Instead
No, I can't refund your money.	"We were not able to refund your money, but we can replace the product at no charge."

   If you think before you speak, you can turn every answer into a positive response.

4. *Avoid scapegoating:*

Forbidden Phrases	What to Say Instead
"That is not my department."	Explain what you can do.
"You're way off base."	"It sounds like you're saying _____."

5. *Avoid crutch words:*

Forbidden Phrases	What to Say Instead
"Ya know," "like," "I guess," "really," "huh…"	(silent pause)

6. *Call attention to people's mistakes indirectly:*

Forbidden Phrases	What to Say Instead
"You didn't do it right."	"There are a few more areas that need to be completed."
"That's definitely wrong."	"Let me see if I've got this straight."

7. *Use "I" messages:*

Forbidden Phrases	What to Say Instead
"You're wrong."	"I can see there's been a miscommunication/misunderstanding."
"You're confusing me."	"I'm confused."
"You're not making any sense."	"Maybe I misunderstood."

8. *Avoid giving orders:*

Forbidden Phrases	What to Say Instead
"You have to…"	Soften the request with phrases like, "You will need to," or "Here is how we can help you with that," or "Will you please."
"You should have done it this way."	"We want your next visit to go as smoothly as possible. This will assist you next time…"

9. *Take responsibility:*

Forbidden Phrases	What to Say Instead
"They will not allow me…"	State what you can do.
"I do not know."	"That's a good question. Let me check and find out."
"We can't do that."	"That's a tough one. Let's see what we can do." Then find an alternative solution.

"It's not my fault/job."   "Let me see what I can do to help."

10. *Avoid causing defensiveness:*

   <u>Forbidden Phrases</u>   <u>What to Say Instead</u>
   "You *never* do it right."   "This form/questionnaire/etc. is not
                                      done correctly."
   "You're *always* late."   "You often/sometimes come in late."
   "You filled this out okay, *but…*" "You filled this out well,…"
   "What's *your* problem?"   "Please tell me what happened."

11. Here are some words and phrases that are guaranteed to bring a smile to your customer's face:

   "Good morning"—or afternoon or evening, said as if you mean it
   "Thank you."
   "Consider it done," "I'll do that immediately," or "I'll take care of that for you."
   "Certainly, sir"—or ma'am, or the individual's name
   "I understand how you feel"—when you do understand
   "I take full responsibility."
   "No problem!"

Appendix 52: Telephone Tips for Excellence

You communicate your attitude, confidence, and competence over the telephone. Exhibiting telephone excellence can be fun, and reap unexpected rewards.

Here's a test: try to remember exactly what the customer said in your most recent telephone conversation. It's pretty hard to do, isn't it?

When you're on the phone, you spend at least half your time listening; however, studies show that most people are poor listeners, and don't retain much of what they hear.

Poor listening habits are not the result of training, but rather the lack of it. Anyone can learn to be a better telephone listener by practicing some basic techniques.

- **Prepare in advance.** Think about the points you want to make, and plan your questions before you pick up the telephone. Planning ahead frees your mind for listening during the call.
- **Practice.** Rehearse with family, friends, and coworkers. Use everyday conversations as a tool for improving your skills.
- **Hold your tongue.** When *you* talk, you don't learn anything new. Be more interested in what the other person has to say. Encourage customers to–talk—the more they tell you about their needs or problems, the easier it will be to find a solution.
- **Concentrate.** Shut out all distractions. Close your ears to everything but the customer. If someone else is competing for your attention, use a hand signal to indicate you are busy. Closing your eyes is another way to focus on the customer.
- **Don't interrupt.** Hear the speaker out. Pause a second or two before you respond. Don't be afraid of a moment of silence. It shows customers that you are thinking about what they said.
- **Take notes.** This will help you remember the important points. But be selective. Trying to write down everything may cause you to miss important details.

- **Ask questions.** If you don't understand something, ask customers to repeat it. This will get them involved in the conversation. Also, ask about their needs, problems, and personal interests. People will perk up about things that they're interested in.
- **Don't jump to conclusions.** Avoid making assumptions about what the speaker is going to say, even if you've heard similar comments and complaints before. Every customer is a unique individual.
- **Visualize the speaker.** Picture the person on the other end. It's easier to become interested in people if you can relate their words to a face.
- **Use conversation** cues. An occasional "Yes," "I see," or "I understand" shows that you are paying attention, and encourages people to keep talking.
- **Listen between the lines.** You can learn a great deal about customers by the way they say things. Pay attention to emotions, not just words. Fear, frustration, and enthusiasm can be easily detected in a person's tone of voice.
- **Identify yourself.** Use your first and last name.
- **Use appropriate volume.** Speak as if someone were two or three feet away.
- **Be clear.** Speak crisply. Avoid slurring syllables or trailing off at the end.
- **Smile.** A smile conveys sincerity and enthusiasm.
- **Speed.** Your speech speed can indicate your attitude. The ideal rate is 150 to 160 words per minute. If you speak faster, the caller may doubt your credibility. Any slower and you may bore your listener. Match the caller's pace.
- **Be expressive.** Be yourself. Speak like you would to a friend.
- **Use positive language.** The words and phrases you use shape other people's images of you. They can affect other people's decisions about whether they are going to cooperate with you. And more importantly, the words that come out of your mouth also go into your ears. Try positive phrases like, "I'd be happy to..." rather than the negative, "I have to..."
- **Lower your volume at the end of a sentence,** especially when asking a question. This conveys confidence and competence. Raising your voice conveys uncertainty.
- **Change the outgoing message daily on your voice mail** or telephone-answering device. Leave a brief, professional message with today's date and when you will be returning calls.

Appendix 53: Common-sense Customer Recovery Strategies

DID YOU KNOW THAT reducing the number of customers who leave by as little as 2% per year is equivalent to the savings generated by cutting costs by 10%?

When you and your employees are faced with angry and complaining customers who threaten to take their business elsewhere, you cannot afford to view these situations as bothersome or only as headaches.

Dealing with angry customers can be an opportunity to find out what needs to be improved in your company, and how to strengthen your customers' loyalty. Listening attentively to those customers, then, represents a real gold mine.

Here's what you can do in your company...

☑Error Recovery

The first step to retaining customers is to create a recovery strategy that you can put in place when errors occur. The key to success in working with angry and complaining customers is to train employees to communicate effectively with these customers. Without adequate training, employees tend to get upset when customers are angry; they don't  know how to handle these situations. Train employees to ask customers:

1. To discuss their problems
2. To listen carefully
3. To offer an apology
4. And, to offer solutions

Most people are happy with a simple apology. It's amazing what an "I'm sorry" will do—because most customers don't hear it very often.

☑Customer Recovery

Next, you need to create a protocol to deal with customers who report that they are leaving.

Conduct an Exit Interview

An exit interview can be conducted either in person or by telephone. During this interview, your task is threefold:

1. Find out why the customer is leaving.
2. Aim to regain the customer's loyalty.
3. Use the information on why the customer is leaving to make improvements to your processes.

You can recover approximately 25% of your lost customers through effective exit interviews and other recovery strategies. You may not be able to recover the remaining 75%. However, the information they can provide on why they're leaving is invaluable. It can help you prevent your current customers from leaving in the future.

Here are the steps you and your employees can take to win customers back...

- ❑ **Express regret.** Begin with something like: "We value your business and are quite upset that you have decided to leave."
- ❑ **Probe for reasons.** "May we ask you why you have decided to leave?" Emphasize that you want to address the problem to keep the customer with the company.
- ❑ **Aim to open communication.** If the person explains that he or she does not want to discuss the problem, rephrase the question differently, along the lines of, "Would you be willing to give us some infor-

mation on where we went wrong so that we don't lose any other customers the same way?"

❏   **Listen carefully and quietly.** The worst thing you can do is to become defensive and argumentative.

❏   **Thank and apologize**. When the customer has finished venting, thank him or her for sharing the information. Then *apologize*. The average employee doesn't know how to say he or she is sorry. Employees are not trained to put themselves in the customer's shoes, and they're not willing to admit mistakes.

Furthermore, employees may be reluctant to take responsibility for a situation and wrongly say to a customer, "It was someone else's fault, not mine," or "I don't know anything about it."

These statements are definitely *not* what customers want to hear—and this is why taking responsibility is so important.

❏   **Find out how to recover**. Now you need to know—directly from the dissatisfied customer—what he or she expects. Ask the customer: "What can we do to make this situation better for you?," or "What can we do to solve this problem for you?"

❏   **Allow the customer to "vent."** He or she needs time to express his or her feelings and get everything off his or her chest.

❏   **Ask for details and make a decision.** Based on the customer's response, you can respond with another question. For example, if the customer reports being dissatisfied with how long it takes to have telephone calls returned, you can say something like, "If we were to implement a process that would guarantee quick return of phone calls, would this encourage you to come back?"

Appendix 54: Cost of Complaints

Ninety-six percent (96%) of your unhappy customers don't complain to you—but they do tell at least ten other people about their problem. Those few who do complain will remain customers if their problem is resolved.

So what does this cost your organization? Here's an interesting exercise on what an "average" customer is worth.

Profit	=	long term profit from a customer
	+	word of mouth to 10 friends
	+	money saved from avoiding the cost of doing it over (response cost)
	–	cost of handling a complaint.

What does it cost to lose customers—the 96% who don't complain to you but who do tell others about you?

Cost	=	what an average customer is worth
	x	how many customers you lose per year (for the average company it's 25% of the customer base)
	+	the cost of the lost potential business from an average of 10 friends of each lost customer.

For example, an average supermarket customer is worth $22,000 over five years. A medium-size market has approximately 1,000 customers. If it loses 25% of its customers per year and each tells at least ten friends, total it up and you're talking about a potential loss of millions of dollars of business.

Appendix 55: Prevent Customer Defection by Crafting a Winback Situation[14]

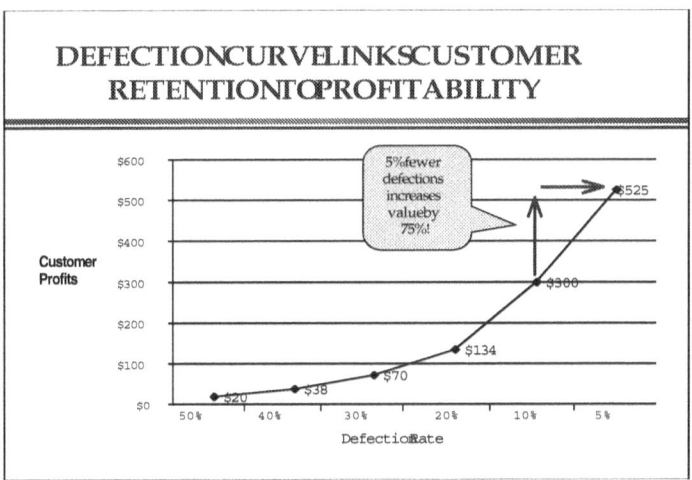

Michael Lowenstein, co-author of *Customer Win-Back: How to Recapture Lost Customers—and Keep Them Loyal* (Jossey-Bass), lists nine suggestions for avoiding customer defection.

Rebuild trust. Improve the quality of your relationship with customers. Customers should identify you with your product or service.

Make your company defection-proof. Constantly evaluate customers' buying habits by establishing purchase metrics from the inception of the relationship. Review what your customer bought at the outset of your relationship, and notice how the pattern has changed over the course of the relationship. Is he/she buying more or less? Is your customer trying your new products? Doing this identifies opportunities for cross-selling and up-selling.

---

14 *Executive Report on Customer Retention*, March 15, 2002

Create an inventory of complaints. You'll often find that customers have the same complaints. Whatever the complaints are, they should be addressed immediately.

Market your products to the right customers. For example, do not target high-income customers with mid-market products. You will just be setting yourself up for customer defection.

Pay attention to your staff, and address their needs as attentively as you would those of your customers. Frederick Reichheld said, "There is direct synaptic connection between the level of employee loyalty and its influence on customer loyalty."

Grade and segment customers who have defected. Assess their second life-time value (SLTV, or value once removed) and their reasons for defection before deciding whether to try to recover the customer.

Thoroughly research the customer's reasons for defection and identify his or her current needs. A customer's defection may have been the result of one complaint or a small number of key issues. These need to be well understood, as do the customer's current requirements (which may have changed since the defection).

Create a plan that reinstates trust and value. When the customer was initially acquired, performance expectations were created. Through some element(s) of under-delivery, trust broke down. The win-back program must reinstate that trust. Companies must address the value message they will convey, the media to be used for communication, the frequency of future communication, alternative strategies, and when the relationship will be retired if conversion is not achieved.

To come up with the most effective plan possible, you'll need to measure, understand, evaluate, and refine it while executing it. Through analysis, you may determine the characteristics of both the plan and the customers who are responding positively to the win-back effort. This insight is used to identify the plan's strengths and weaknesses, and target and refine messages.

Appendix 56: Avoidable Upsets

The annoyances you have some responsibility causing are:

1. **You or someone in your organization promised something that was not delivered.**

   - If you promised the customer you would get back to him and you didn't, then he may become upset. With good reason. Most of us become upset when people promise action and don't follow through.

2. **You or someone in your organization was indifferent, rude, or discourteous to a customer.**

   - Many times discourtesy is unintentional. You may not have thought about your statement before you blurted it out. Some people try to make funny comments, but these may come across as rude. Treat every customer as a special aunt or uncle.

3. **A customer feels you or someone else in your organization had an unpleasant attitude toward him.**

   - Perhaps a customer was surly himself, dressed unusually, or treated you poorly. However, you always need to treat customers supremely well.

4. **A customer doesn't feel that he/she was listened to.**

   - People want to be listened to. They don't want to have to repeat themselves.

5. **A customer was told he/she has no right to be angry.**

   - Everyone has a right to his or her emotions. Telling a customer otherwise will just intensify the anger.

6. **The customer gave a smart or flip reply.**

   • Sarcastic remarks only heighten anger; they seldom ease tension.

7. **A customer is embarrassed at doing something incorrectly.**

   • Make sure the customer understands what he/she needs to know before he/she uses your product or service. Go over any procedures about returns or guarantees beforehand. That way you'll have fewer customers who are angry because of a misunderstanding.

8. **A customer's integrity or honesty has been questioned.**

   • Treat customers with respect and dignity, like your favorite aunt or uncle. If there is a problem, assume your organization has made the mistake until shown otherwise. Instead of "You didn't pay us," say, "We don't have a record of receiving your payment. Would you be kind enough to see if your check cleared the bank?"
   • Work to eliminate body language, voice tone, or facial expressions that convey distrust. Avoid projecting an "us versus them" attitude about customers.
   • Never call a customer a deadbeat, liar, cheat, thief, etc. Never threaten a customer.

9. **You or someone in your organization argued with the customer.**

   • As Dale Carnegie said: "The only way to get the best of an argument is to avoid it." This is especially true with customers. If you argue with a customer you always lose—even if you win the argument. It's not good for the other customers to witness an argument. They won't like seeing you treat a customer poorly, whether or not the customer was in the wrong.

Appendix 57: Reasons Companies Fail to Hear the Voice of the Customer

Spending hundreds of thousands of dollars on research to hear the voice of the customer is not uncommon. Why, then, do companies fail to hear what customers are saying? Richard Whiteley and Diane Hessan of the Forum Corporation have observed these top eight reasons.

1. No one is assigned overall responsibility. Each part of the company collects the data it thinks it needs, and no one ever integrates it into a coherent picture.

2. There is no systematic effort. The idea that everyone should be involved in collecting customer data is allowed to result in uncontrolled duplication with no coordinated analysis. There is too much confusing "noise".

3. The wrong tools are used. Collecting demographic statistics on your customers may be interesting, but those statistics are almost useless in zeroing in on what customers really expect and will pay for. They tell who and where your customers are, but not what they want.

4. Data is gathered only from some customers. No one has adequately segmented the customer population. The voice you are amplifying reflects the actual needs of only a small fraction of the people you want to serve.

5. Data on customer satisfaction is gathered, but it is not compared with customer expectations or other measures that help prioritize issues.

6. Non-customers who can articulate the needs of real and potential customers are not included. Salespeople, service providers, lost customers, lost prospects and competitors' customers need to be heard from, too.

7. Information is not shared throughout the organization. Someone in the organization may know what the customer wants, but this information never reaches the people controlling what the customer gets.

8. Information is shared but sparsely used. Managers collect binders full of survey data, but few take any action based on the information.

Appendix 58: "At Risk" Customer Profile[15]

Using these processes to learn from past defections and implementing basic systems for monitoring relationships, companies are equipped to conduct simple (yet significantly more educated) analyses of current customers to assess the likelihood of defection.

Company A can leverage analysis of past defectors to conduct simple evaluation of current customers' statistics

How closely do the customer's general characteristics fit the profile of at-risk customers?

Static Characteristics
θ Less than 18 months as customer
θ Less than $5,000 annual premium
θ Customer's business has profit margin of less than 5%
θ Has switched agencies more than once in past three years

Has the customer been experiencing typical drivers of customer defection?

Drivers of Defections	
Controllable	**Uncontrollable**
θ More than 20% of claims payouts have been late	θ Larger (non-customer) company plans to acquire customer
θ 5% of invoices have contained errors	θ Customer's market share has dropped more than half (due to success of new entrants)
θ Customer account has been transferred to "green" sales representative	θ Competitor has introduced appealing, low-cost new products

15 Corporate Executive Board, Sales Executive Council Executive Inquiry, "Understanding Customer Retention, Part III: Customer Defection Risk Analysis, June 1998, p. 29.

Is the customer exhibiting behavior that historically precedes defection?

Pre-Defection Warning Signs

θ   Customer has canceled more than two coverages

θ   Number of complaints to customer service center has increased more than 30%

θ   Multiple claim losses have occurred

Appendix 59: Characteristics of Defectors vs. Non-Defectors

To create a more reliable defector profile, Company A must establish that these selected attributes differentiate defectors from the remaining (loyal) customer base. In this example, Company A adds a column that tracks these characteristics among **non**-defectors.

Company A compares characteristics of defectors and non-defectors to identify strongest correlations[16]

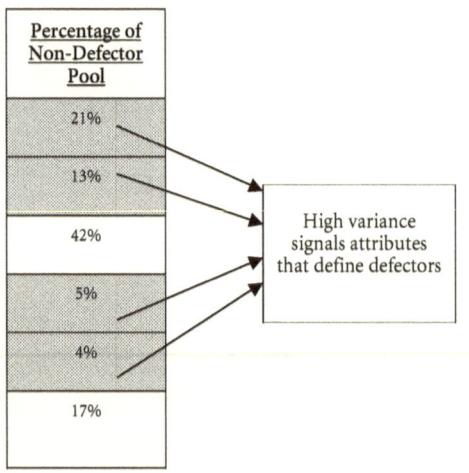

	Characteristic	Percentage of Defector Pool	Percentage of Non-Defector Pool
θ	Less than $5,000 in monthly shipments	82%	21%
θ	Less than 18 months as customer	69%	13%
θ	Served by salesperson with less than two years of tenure	44%	42%
θ	Customer's business has profit margin of less than 5%	31%	5%
θ	Switched suppliers more than once in past five years	28%	4%
θ	Located more that 50 miles from nearest distribution center	16%	17%

High variance signals attributes that define defectors

---

16 Corporate Executive Board, Sales Executive Council Executive Inquiry, "Understanding Customer Retention, Part III: Customer Defection Risk Analysis," June 1998.

As these comparisons illustrate, the characteristics with greatest variance between the defector and non-defector pools are those that most strongly indicate defection proclivity. It follows that companies should disregard characteristics that are representative of the entire customer base or that do not vary significantly from the retention behavior of other customers.

Once it has determined the traits that most clearly differentiate defectors from other customers, Company A can create a profile of the generic at-risk customer. This "snapshot" emphasizes the qualities of customers that will make them fundamentally more difficult for Company A to retain, distinct from any developments in its relationships with these customers.

Appendix 60: Early Defection Warning Signs

Six signs that a good worker is about to quit–and what to do about it
CNNfn
by The Applegate Group
July 08, 1999

NEW YORK (CNNFN)—The flush U.S. economy continues to be more and more of a bittersweet blessing for small business owners, who are feeling the squeeze of the tight labor market as never before.

While big business is also caught in the crunch, small companies—which cannot offer the salaries, benefit packages and bonus incentives that are de rigueur in today's competitive job market—face even steeper challenges.

But there are ways to dam the exodus of valuable employees, says Diane Domeyer, executive director of Office Team, a Menlo Park, California-based temporary-employment firm.

Domeyer, whose firm specializes in placing administrative staff, says employees often wave "farewell flags" long before they jump ship, and that smart employers can detect and address these warning signs before it's too late:

- **Going solo.** If a once-active contributor to group projects is suddenly taking a back seat, the person may be keeping a low profile while they line up a new job.
- **Changing patterns.** If a usually orderly employee seems to have lost their knack for organization, they may no longer have a reason to be concerned about their office appearance.
- **Dapper Dan.** A normally casual employee showing up for work in a suit and tie may be all dressed up with some place to go—like a lunch-time job interview.
- **Stretching personal time.** Longer lunch hours, requests for additional vacation days, or time off with little notice could all indicate an employee needs free time for career research, job interviews, or even meetings at his or her new job.

- **The click off.** Employees using the Internet, printer or fax machine to conduct job searches or send out resumes may seem over-protective or guarded about the materials on their desk—or be quick to click off their computer screens when you enter their work area.
- **Phone fiend.** An employee whose phone use has noticeably increased may be setting up interviews or negotiating offers.

If you notice some or all of the above warning signs at your company, Domeyer advises taking action while the "farewell flags" are only at half mast.

You may be surprised to find that an employee's job dissatisfaction has less to do with money than with finding the work rewarding or their efforts appreciated.

"Managers must constantly provide the intellectual challenge and recognition necessary to retain key employees," Domeyer said. "This is particularly true of administrative staff who have become pivotal in an increasingly fast-paced environment, and whose technical skills are highly marketable."

Of course, employers should also be aware that the above warning signs might not point to a job hunt, but to a variety of personal or professional problems that an employee may be facing.

Domeyer says that's all the more reason for employers to be sensitive to behavioral changes in employees, and to address problems immediately.

"It's preferable to act quickly based on your observations rather than to see a talented person leave," she said.

(Syndicated columnist Jane Applegate covers small business for CNNfn.com. Applegate, author of 201 Great Ideas for Your Small Business and a business owner herself, also maintains the site janeapplegate.com to help her fellow entrepreneurs.)

0-595-29719-6

www.ingramcontent.com/pod-product-compliance
Lightning Source LLC
Chambersburg PA
CBHW030929180526
45163CB00002B/508